HUNTER S. THOMPSON

HUNTER S. THOMPSON
THE LAST INTERVIEW

and OTHER CONVERSATIONS

edited and with an introduction by DAVID STREITFELD

MELVILLE HOUSE
BROOKLYN · LONDON

HUNTER S. THOMPSON: THE LAST INTERVIEW AND OTHER CONVERSATIONS

First Melville House printing: February 2018

"Fantasy and Reality: Life with the Angels" is from a lightly edited radio interview conducted by Studs Terkel of WFMT Radio in Chicago, March 1967. Courtesy of the Studs Terkel Radio Archive.

"Your Worst Fears *Always* Come True" by Henry Allen © 1972 by Henry Allen. First published in *The Washington Post Book Week*, July 23, 1972.

"You had to get into journalism just to keep up with the madness" is from a lightly edited radio interview conducted by Studs Terkel of WFMT Radio in Chicago, March 14, 1973. Courtesy of the Studs Terkel Radio Archive.

"Political Highs and Lows" by Jane Perlez © 1979 by Jane Perlez. First published in the *Washington Journalism Review* in November/December 1979.

"The Doctor Is In" by Curtis Wilkie © 1988 by Curtis Wilkie. First published in *The Boston Globe Magazine* on January 7, 1988.

"I *enjoy* drugs" is excerpted from *Hunter S. Thompson* by William McKeen (Twayne, 1991). © 1991 by William McKeen.

"This is not a night to be alone" © 2018 by David Streitfeld.

"Fear and Loathing After 9/11" was originally broadcast on *The Media Report*, a program on Australian Broadcasting Corp. Radio National network. August 29, 2002.

"A Downhill, Hellbound Train" by Jessica Hopsicker. © 2004 by Jessica Hopsicker. First published in *The College Crier* magazine, October 2004.

Melville House Publishing		8 Blackstock Mews
46 John Street	and	Islington
Brooklyn, NY 11201		London N4 2BT

mhpbooks.com
facebook.com/mhpbooks
@melvillehouse

ISBN: 978-1-61219-693-0

Printed in the United States of America
10 9 8 7 6 5 4 3 2

A catalog record for this book is available from the Library of Congress.

CONTENTS

INTRODUCTION

DAVID STREITFELD

I once spent many agonizing minutes watching Hunter Thompson, who liked to boast that he could use the English language as both a musical instrument and a political weapon, trying to sign his name.

This was in late 1990, in a hotel room in New York City. A publicist asked him to autograph his latest book before she left, a little souvenir of hours spent trying to get the writer to do the most basic things, like get out of bed. Hunter would start writing, get distracted, pause, gather his wits, stare at his hand as if it were an alien life form, throw something. I thought, *Signed books by this guy must be really scarce.*

A few decades later, with Gonzo nostalgia in full swing, eBay was auctioning a signed copy of *Generation of Swine* or *Songs of the Doomed* nearly every day, usually with just the scribbled letters "HST." Collectors sometimes bid hundreds of dollars. Most of the autographs must be fake, but probably a few are real. At this point, who can tell the difference?

It's been almost half a century since the work that made Hunter's name and more than a decade since his suicide, but he was so controversial, so denounced, and so celebrated that the smoke still hasn't cleared. He was influential and entertaining, everyone must give him that, but did he ever become the artist that he so palpably longed to be? Was he a madman, or was he a writer who played a role and got trapped in it? Did his prodigious intake of drugs and alcohol weaken his work, or make it possible in the first place? Like most of the great American writers, he did his best work first; is his life a tragedy of blown opportunities and persistent decline, or fundamentally a success?

Hunter himself was plagued by doubt, and other opinions were sharply divided. Tom Wolfe, who worked some of the same territory, called him "the greatest comic writer of the twentieth century." But Hunter's first wife, Sandy, who made his career possible in so many ways, said, "Hunter wanted to be a great writer and he had the genius, the talent, and, early on, the will and the means. He was horrified by whom he had become and ashamed—or I really should say tortured. He knew he had failed."

That's pretty harsh. Few writers achieve the hallowed groves of immortality, and those that do follow different roads. Hawthorne, Melville, Gabriel García Márquez, and Nabokov made it on their work alone. Mark Twain, Oscar Wilde, F. Scott Fitzgerald, Hemingway, and Kerouac all found that the stories they wrote merged with the story they lived, and so did Hunter. It happened gradually but inexorably. The first edition of *Hell's Angels* from 1967 has a picture of a member of the biker gang on the cover. The Modern Library edition, printed thirty years later, bears a photo of Hunter, who always made clear he was not an Angel.

One of Hunter's biographers, William McKeen, calls him "the favorite writer for many people who didn't read books." He stands in front of his work, often obscuring it. The books about him, including a half-dozen full-scale biographies, outnumber the books he wrote. There are movies (both Bill Murray and Johnny Depp played Hunter, not very successfully), documentaries, memoirs, comic books, lavish oversized reprints designed for the coffee table rather than the shelves, even a memorial beer. The original work is scarcely necessary, which seems a shame, because we need it more than ever.

These are tumultuous times. The country is on edge, unable to look away from what is going on in Washington. Hunter loved moments like this. The thing he hated the most was boredom, and no one is bored now. The thing he loved the most was politics, which continually disappointed him but which he couldn't let go of. His great nemesis was Richard Nixon. Douglas Brinkley, a friend and historian, said, "Hunter hated Nixon so much he loved him." In the Age of Trump, we're all Hunter Thompson.

Hunter would have done more than relish the current scene; he would have realized how we got here. Indeed, he predicted it. After hanging out with the Hells Angels, the writer concluded that they were not "some romantic leftover" but "the first wave of a future that nothing in our history has prepared us to cope with."

As he told Studs Terkel in 1967, the Angels were the vanguard of the masses rejected by technology, by progress, by history:

> The people who are being left out and put behind won't be obvious for years. And Christ only knows what'll happen when it's 1985. There will be a million Hell's Angels. They won't be wearing the colors but they'll be people who are looking for vengeance because they've been left behind.

It took rather longer than Hunter thought, but that pretty much nails the millions of voters who put Trump over the top in 2016. There were so many more people out there looking for vengeance—social, personal, political, economic—than anyone realized.

American politics is always circling back to its past. The Trump/Clinton face-off has curious parallels to the 1972 election. Richard Nixon, Hunter noted, said the voting that year would offer "the clearest choice of this century." Nixon was right but not in the way he meant.

"It is Nixon himself who represents that dark, venal and incurably violent side of the American character almost every country in the world has learned to fear and despise," Hunter wrote. "Our Barbie-doll president, with his Barbie-doll wife and his boxful of Barbie-doll children is also America's answer to the monstrous Mr. Hyde. He speaks for the Werewolf in us; the bully, the predatory shyster who turns into something unspeakable, full of claws and bleeding string-warts on nights when the moon comes too close . . ."

Americans chose the dark side in 1972 and did so again in 2016. We like to go up to the edge, daring ourselves not to fall in. Hunter recognized the impulse because it was the same one he lived by. He insisted on amping things up, putting the entire bet on one role of the dice.

A favorite anecdote: somewhere in the early seventies, *Rolling Stone* writer David Felton went to visit Hunter at a California hotel. The inventor of Gonzo journalism "had a leer on his face and he was just slamming the door to his apartment as hard as he could, over and over again until it practically came off the hinges," Felton told a biographer.

"He would slam it and then he would smile and open it; and he'd slam it again. It was because the guy upstairs complained about the noise. And Hunter's theory on those things, which he's done many times, is that if somebody complains about the noise you turn it up, not down, and they'll stop complaining eventually."

This was the reason why Hunter was placed on this earth: to make everyone realize how far you can go when you're going too far. He was provocative without even trying. It's a shame he never made it to Twitter. His quips—"I think having a favorite baseball team is like having a favorite oil company" is one of my favorites—would have launched a thousand flame wars.

But if Hunter is amazingly contemporary in some ways, in others he already seems as distant as Edith Wharton. Take, for instance, his love of drugs and alcohol.

The first time Hunter ever took LSD was during a

legendary moment of the sixties, when the Hells Angels partied with Ken Kesey, author of *One Flew Over the Cuckoo's Nest* and budding countercultural guru, and his Merry Prankster buddies. This happened in La Honda, a wooded community in the hills just south of San Francisco. Hunter was working on *Hell's Angels* and made the introductions. The Pranksters, heavily into acid, offered some to the Angels. Hunter feared the worst—forty Angels unleashed!—and so naturally decided the only thing to do was to get fucked up himself.

An 800-microgram dose "almost blew my head off," he said, but in a really good way. Hunter had heard stories about a psychiatrist who tripped "and wound up running naked through the streets of Palo Alto, screaming that he wanted to be punished for his crimes. He didn't know what his crimes were and nobody else did, either, so they took him away and he spent a long time in a loony bin somewhere, and I thought, 'That's not what *I* need,'" he told *Playboy*.

His dark fear was that, if he lost control, "all these horrible psychic worms and rats would come out. But I went to the bottom of the well and found out there's nothing down there I have to worry about."

He was liberated. In his house in Woody Creek, Colorado, he pinned up this admonition: "Life should not be a journey to the grove with the intention of arriving safely in a pretty and well-preserved body, but rather to skid into the broadside in a cloud of smoke, thoroughly used up and worn out and loudly proclaiming, 'What a ride!'"

Here's a paradox for you: even as the nation slouches toward legalization of marijuana—a drug, as it happens, that

Hunter didn't have much use for—the age of the wild writer is dead and buried. The only time anyone ever admits to getting ripped is in a recovery memoir. So no one will ever again write a book that opens like *Las Vegas*, with a full-throated yowl of exuberance:

> We were somewhere around Barstow on the edge
> of the desert when the drugs began to take hold. I
> remember saying something like, "I feel a bit light-
> headed; maybe you should drive . . ." And suddenly
> there was a terrible roar all around us and the sky
> was full of what looked like huge bats, all swooping
> and screeching and diving around the car, which
> was going about a hundred miles an hour with the
> top down to Las Vegas. And a voice was screaming:
> "Holy Jesus! What are these goddamn animals?"

The problem was that Hunter required extreme stimulus to do the work. He needed to feel his nerves tingling. "Your method of research is to tie yourself to a railroad track when you know a train is coming to it, and see what happens," his editor, Jim Silberman, told him.

The result was that when the news dried up, so did he. In 1978, looking back a decade, he said, "There's nothing that menacing and tangible to grab right now. I can recall almost all through the sixties, I'd wake up every morning in a black rage every time I saw a newspaper . . . Every time you turned around, the candidate you were counting on to save the world had his head blown off right in front of you . . . You had just a little bit of rest before someone else was killed."

Ah, Hunter. People are being killed again on the streets. The world is a mess. Nixon was a model of restraint compared to the current occupant of the White House. Would that you were around to cover it.

He was literally stronger and certainly crazier than any writer I've ever met, and I've met a lot of them. Around 1993 or so, I seized an opportunity to get to the bottom of Hunter. Three full-scale biographies appeared at the same time. He wasn't even dead. This was a surprise to the writers, who naturally didn't like it. They took the opportunity to take shots at each other. I quizzed them all for clues to the mystery.

The most flamboyant of the books was by E. Jean Carroll, who styled herself as a sort of female Hunter. Her book, *Hunter*, featured excellent anecdotes from the crowd that populated the writer's life, like this from a friend named David Burgin:

> Hunter had driven down in his new Volvo. About three days later he called me up and he wanted to know where his car was. And I said, "Your car? I don't know where your car is. Where'd you leave it?" And he said, "Well, I was at the Star." And I said, "Jesus, Hunter, that was *three* days ago." And he said, "My dogs are in it."

No one would tell a tale like that about themselves today, or even tell it about someone else; they would be denounced by animal rights activists or at least deemed heartless. But note too that we don't actually know if it is true. It is a story in every sense of the word.

Carroll was very smart on Hunter, summing him up like this: "It's quite hard on Hunter having to be Hunter. But basically, he is Hunter and acts like that anyway." Unfortunately, her oral history was interspersed with truly excruciating soft-core porn chapters about a fictional alter-ego, Miss Laetitia Snap, who is kidnapped by the writer. The goal was to get the reader of *Hunter* to experience what he was really like, but only Hunter could successfully go Gonzo.

Miss Snap's amorous encounters with Hunter were rooted in real life. Carroll said this gave *Hunter* an advantage. Other writers, she suggested, "don't really know who Hunter really is. Ask them who his present girlfriend is. Who sees him before he goes to bed? What's he like in bed?"

The other biographers, both men who had some personal experience with Hunter but never slept with him, took offense at this.

"I don't know if David McCullough, who wrote that Harry Truman biography, ever knew him. But I know one thing—he never slept with him. Objectivity has its merits in doing a good biography. Subjectivity has real limitations," said Peter Whitmer, author of *When the Going Gets Weird*.

Paul Perry, author of *Fear and Loathing: The Strange and Terrible Saga of Hunter S. Thompson*, chimed in, "I don't know what he's like in bed. But I think there's a cardinal rule of journalism: you don't fuck your sources. I got my information the old-fashioned way. I stood up and did my interviews."

What was Thompson's own opinion about all of this? When I tracked him down, he sounded alternately reconciled to the books ("I've taken a lot of flogging over the years, and I suppose it goes with the territory.") and pissed off ("They get in the way. It's like people throwing gravel or ball bearings at you when you're trying to work.").

The biographers didn't agree about Hunter's prospects as a writer, either. Perry took the conventional view: "I hate to say it, but after 1985 Hunter kind of died for me in a lot of ways. He hasn't produced anything worth a damn. This is a guy who rode drugs and alcohol to his own peak, and now he's ridden drugs and alcohol to the bottom." Carroll and Whitmer were more forgiving.

All these years later, there is still no consensus on Hunter. Sometimes I think we will never come to grips with him until we arrive at some conclusions about his perennial topic, the Death of the American Dream. "To hell with the American Dream," he said in 1977. "Let's write it off as a suicide." But he just couldn't. Neither could most people, because it was just too bleak a conclusion. We're still arguing about it, now more than ever.

Let's give Hunter the last word. In 2003, an interviewer for *Salon* asked him if the Dream had been on its deathbed since 1968.

HUNTER: I think that's right.

SALON: A lot of people would argue with you about that anyway, and believe that the American Dream is alive and well.

HUNTER: They need to take a better look around.

SALON: But in a way, haven't you lived the American Dream?

HUNTER: Goddamnit! *[Pause.]* I haven't thought about it that way. I suppose you could say in a certain way I have.

Hunter had a lot of friends, many of whom were in the media, and he loved to talk—it was a way of both energizing himself for work and putting it off. As a result, there were a lot of interviews over the years, with more of them still surfacing from buried archives, like the chats with Studs Terkel in this book. He was always good copy but sometimes hard to follow. He liked to mutter and often wandered into obscure conversational thickets. In the transcriptions of the radio interviews reprinted here, his comments have been edited without, I hope, distorting his meaning.

When he killed himself in 2005, he had just published a book, which he had gamely tried to publicize. There were several contenders for the last interview. The one featured here has a good claim to actually being it. Hunter was frustrated with the questions—the youthful reporter had never interviewed anyone before—but still very engaged. There was little sense that he was weary enough to end his life within six months.

But then, that was Hunter's point: he wanted to go out on his own terms, and he did. He died the way he lived. In that way, at least, he was completely authentic. What a ride!

FANTASY AND REALITY: LIFE WITH THE ANGELS

INTERVIEW BY STUDS TERKEL
THE STUDS TERKEL PROGRAM
MARCH, 1967

Excerpts from a radio interview conducted by Studs Terkel of WFMT Radio in Chicago.

STUDS TERKEL: Hells Angels—the name itself evokes a variety of emotions. During World War I they were heroes, aviators, but the Hells Angels today represent something else, don't they? A certain kind of motorcycle gang. There's a book by Hunter S. Thompson, a very powerful book. In fact, I think Hunter Thompson, our guest, is a new kind of journalist, and I say may his tribe increase. He's the journalist who is not detached, who doesn't observe his phenomenon from a distance but becomes involved. In fact, he was almost an honorary member of the Hells Angels, you might say. We'll hear about that. Or a dishonored member. Subtitled *The Strange and Terrible Saga of the Outlaw Motorcycle Gangs*, it's a book that is important in its implications about our society.

STUDS TERKEL: It's not a question of moralizing about good or bad guys. The question of *Hell's Angels* is "inarticulate" and "violent." You used these two words, didn't you?

HUNTER S. THOMPSON: Yeah.

TERKEL: Inarticulate and violent.

THOMPSON: Well?

TERKEL: Who are the men you've known? You speak of a great number of these guys throughout. There's the leader who is now celebrated —

THOMPSON: Some are very articulate.

TERKEL: Hmmmm?

THOMPSON: Barger.

TERKEL: Sonny Barger, their leader.

THOMPSON: Sonny is very articulate. I remember a press conference he called when he sent that telegram to President Johnson volunteering their services in Vietnam. As gorillas.

TERKEL: Yeah.

THOMPSON: Animals. G-O-R, gorillas. He was totally poised in front of forty-two reporters and I forgot how many cameras and the TV dollies.

TERKEL: Is it because now he has become a celebrated figure?

THOMPSON: No, I think he could have been articulate in just about anything he decided to do. But given his temperament, if he went to work in a factory he'd probably stuff the foreman's head down an airshaft.

TERKEL: What makes a man join Hells Angels? Perhaps we should get down to specifics. There are similar groups. In Chicago there's a group called the Outlaws who say they are tougher than the Hells Angels. There are several branches. They're called one-percenters, aren't they?

THOMPSON: Well the AMA called them one-percenters.

TERKEL: The American Motorcyclist Association.

THOMPSON: The AMA is the sporting competition arm of a much larger trade association for bikes and scooters and almost anything with two wheels and a motor. The AMA is a motorcycle lobby, really. They sponsor all these races around the country and some of them pretty big, but they don't like the image the Hells Angels have given the motorcycle. So at one point they came out with a statement saying, "Don't believe all this bad stuff you hear about motorcycles. It's only one percent of bikers." So the Angels, with their pattern of adopting disparaging remarks, picked it up and were proud of being the dirty evil one percent. So now they all wear this triangular patch.

TERKEL: It's a patch called one-percenters.

THOMPSON: Yeah.

TERKEL: On the cover of *Hell's Angels* is a shot of the back of a long-haired member of Hells Angels. A patch of a skull with wings: Hells Angels. And there's a one, for the one percent.

THOMPSON: That little thing, yes.

TERKEL: This is the outside-the-pale-of-respectability group.

THOMPSON: All across the country, all the other motorcycle gangs, they don't want to be called a gang. They call themselves a club. But all the other motorcycle clubs, even the Outlaws, defer to the Angels being No. 1. There's a group in the east called the Pagans that claim two or three times the membership of the Angels. And they say they want to take over the East Coast like the Angels have taken over the West Coast. That's their concept. The Angels have taken over the West Coast.

TERKEL: It's almost as though a syndicate were at work, saying this is my turf and this is your turf.

•   •   •

TERKEL: Why are the Hells Angels this kind of group? You speak of foul fighting; they stomp someone. You were stomped. Violence for the sake of violence.

THOMPSON: It's bylaw either No. 10 or 11. It says when an Angel punches a non-Angel, other Angels will participate. So I was a victim of bylaw No. 10 or 11. I should've known that. It was a lapse of caution.

TERKEL: This is not Queensberry rules?

THOMPSON: All necessary participation, as far as it goes.

TERKEL: Kicking, gouging.

THOMPSON: Oh, that's elementary.

TERKEL: Yeah.

THOMPSON: During my stomping, I could see the guy who'd originally teed off on me, from nowhere with no warning, circling around with a rock about twelve inches long—it must have weighed twenty pounds—trying to get at me to crash it down in my head. That was my main worry. I tried to keep my eyes on him because I didn't want to have my skull fractured. That sounds bad, talking about it now, but the Angels wouldn't have seen anything unusual in it.

TERKEL: We hear more and more of senseless violence, and throughout the book your observations are about more than the Angels, they're about our society. It's since World War II, isn't it, that this phenomenon has come to be?

THOMPSON: I think the Angels came out of World War II, and not just the Angels themselves but this whole alienated and violent subculture of people wandering around looking for either an opportunity or, if not an opportunity, then vengeance for not getting an opportunity. Because they get to be thirty and suddenly they wake up one morning and they realize there are no more chances, it's all gone. "Yeah," they say, "I've been an outlaw for ten years or twelve years." By this time, they've been in jail a few times or maybe the pen. And it makes them very bitter. The older ones are generally much more bitter than the younger ones because the younger ones have options, they can quit. At least they have the illusion of being able to quit and go straight. But the older they get, the more they lose their illusions and that makes them meaner.

TERKEL: Yeah.

THOMPSON: They want to get back at the people who put them in this terrible dead-end tunnel.

TERKEL: Who are these people they want to get back at?

THOMPSON: It's kind of "they." Paranoid. It's you, it's me, it's whoever might come too close on the highway. It's somebody who makes a remark in a bar. The Angels call them "the citizens." Anybody who looks respectable, looks like he isn't doomed—like he has some kind of option or money or a home. All the things they don't have.

TERKEL: Do you sense that they really want to be respectable in the sense of having that home and those possessions?

THOMPSON: Well, they did at one time. It's hard to say. You have to kind of treat it individually.

TERKEL: Yeah.

THOMPSON: But they get to a point when they realize they can't have them, that they don't have these opportunities anymore to make it in the Great Society. Once this realization comes then it makes them resent these things even more. It's like the one-percenter patch.

TERKEL: Yeah.

THOMPSON: The AMA saw it as a derogatory thing. The Angels adopted it as a positive thing.

TERKEL: Your book is an excellent one, but there have been write-ups in the mass media that were considered bad publicity. They would rather have that than no publicity, wouldn't they?

THOMPSON: Oh absolutely. They would die right away with no publicity. There'd be no reason for being in the club.

TERKEL: Now they're recognized even though they are the enemy, quote-unquote. They're recognized as somebody.

THOMPSON: Well, it's the recognition that makes up for all their deprivation.

TERKEL: So these are the losers in our society who won't be passive losers. As outlaws, they become active.

THOMPSON: That's why they appeal to people who are passive losers. All the people who would like to take a big rock and crash it down on the finance company–manager's head can watch movies of the Hells Angels or read about them getting vengeance on all the people who have wronged them.

•   •   •

TERKEL: We have technology, we have the computer, we have labor-saving devices. We have the need for more and more college education for almost any kind of job. And you have this tremendous mass of young who find themselves obsolete, almost.

THOMPSON: The Angels, most of them, found themselves obsolete years ago. So the people who are the Hells Angels that are being created now probably won't be obvious for another five years. It takes a while to cultivate that kind of bitterness—where, when somebody calls you a dirty bum, you don't look in the mirror and think, maybe I should wash my face. You go out and rub scum on you and get dirtier. Then you go back in and punch him and break a bottle and stick it in his gut. So we won't see what what's happening today. The people who are being left out and put behind won't be obvious for years. And Christ only knows what'll happen when it's 1985. There will be a million Hells Angels. They won't be wearing the colors but they'll be people who are looking for vengeance because they've been left behind.

TERKEL: That which was considered derogatory becomes, as you point out, a badge of honor.

THOMPSON: Yeah.

TERKEL: They take this very thing, the obscenities and all, and it becomes their way of life.

THOMPSON: They like to throw it back in your face and say, Yeah sir, I am a dirty bum, I'm even dirtier than you thought. And I'm also going to punish you for calling me that and making me that, and making me that too.

• • •

TERKEL: Angels bring out this violence in other people.

THOMPSON: The Angels claim that they don't look for trouble, they just try to live peaceful lives and be left alone. But on the other hand, they go out and put themselves into situations deliberately and constantly that are either going to humiliate somebody else or cause them to avoid humiliation by fighting. I've seen them countless times put people in situations where they have to either crawl or fight, almost by just being there and smiling at them. And of course, they live in a world that isn't as polite as the world a lot of people live in . . . They need their fantasy of being tough.

TERKEL: The fantasy and the reality.

THOMPSON: Without the fantasy they couldn't face the reality, because it's too horrible. Every day they wake up and their teeth hurt more and no dentist will touch them without payment in advance. That sort of thing. So their reality is really pretty bad, and their fantasy is all they have left. This fantasy of being big and tough and powerful and right against all these people who are wrong and evil and going to push down on them, bend them.

TERKEL: This myth is necessary because the reality is so bleak and so joyless.

THOMPSON: Well the myth is as necessary to the Angels as it is to *Time* and *Newsweek*, because in order to see the Angels for what they are, as a sort of reflection of President Johnson's foreign policy, then you'd have to really think about it. You'd have to see that we're breeding Hells Angels on every street corner. They just don't wear the jackets yet. So it's much easier to consider them an isolated oddity. It's much easier to see them as something that came out of some past Gypsy culture, dying out because they can't proliferate or breed anymore. That isn't that the case. I think the world will have ten times as many Hells Angels in ten years as we do now.

•   •   •

TERKEL: We come back again to the mass media—*Time, Life, Newsweek, Saturday Evening Post.* The mass media and the creatures they create. Hells Angels, they say, is part of a Gypsy tradition, nothing to do with our society. And you come back again and again in the book and prove it's very much part of the fabric of our society since World War II.

THOMPSON: I think it is. And after writing this book I'm much more conscious of it. I'm much more conscious of the kind of anger that lurks everywhere. Chicago, L.A.—almost any urban situation. I used to get in a lot of brawls in bars. Good fun things, everybody would get up and have a drink afterwards. I keep my mouth shut now. I've turned into a professional coward.

TERKEL: Professional coward?

THOMPSON: Yeah, because there's too many really mean angry people out there.

TERKEL: Yes.

THOMPSON: I'm not. I'm not looking just to mash somebody's head and get back at the world. In conjunction with this I somehow got mixed up in a lot of karate classes, with karate people. Talk about seething vengeance. A lot of the Angels are big on karate because it's like the motorcycle. Here's a powerful thing and it's safe. Carrying a gun is not safe for anybody with a criminal record or who is likely to get stopped. But karate is really booming on the West Coast.

TERKEL: That's interesting. It's probably booming here too.

THOMPSON: Yeah.

TERKEL: This is interesting, the karate classes and the chop that can kill a man.

THOMPSON: It's much harder to learn than that. I've gone through just enough of it to know that it isn't a matter of going in and learning a secret chop. Mainly it's a matter of conditioning. But the Angels see it as something that they can have to give them even more power over the squares and citizens. Like the bike. Anybody who has any kind of sensuality in them at all would recognize what the Angels call screwing it on, getting a big bike and just running it flat out as fast as it'll go. I used to take mine out at night on the Coast Highway. Just drunk out of my mind. Rode it for twenty and thirty miles in short pants and a t-shirt. It's a beautiful feeling.

TERKEL: Power. Power and freedom too.

THOMPSON: I recognize it as an illusion and a fantasy. I enjoy it, but I sort of know where I am when I'm doing it. But for somebody who has nothing else to go back to, this is maybe one of the happiest minutes of his life. And you can imagine if that's true just how powerful he'd feel if he could give you one of these *[karate chop vocal effect]*—

TERKEL: Yeah.

THOMPSON: —in the head. It's not a chop, it's a head snap.

TERKEL: So you'll have that physical power with your fist with karate or with the motorcycle.

THOMPSON: It's like carrying a gun.

TERKEL: And inside you is this tremendous joylessness and frustration of—

THOMPSON: —wanting—

TERKEL: —being the loser.

THOMPSON: Wanting to get even.

TERKEL: So the combination is pretty lethal, is it not, in our society?

THOMPSON: Oh, Christ. It is.

TERKEL: And you say that you find it more and more.

THOMPSON: Or maybe I'm just more aware of it. I'm not sure whether I'm seeing more because after a year of drinking in taverns in Oakland, you really see a different side. At least for me, it's a different side of the world. Everybody's mean. People come in and they leave their bars in the guns. These aren't Hells Angels.

TERKEL: Yeah.

THOMPSON: What am I saying? They leave their guns in the bars. You got in my head. People are coming—

TERKEL: These are not Hells Angels?

THOMPSON: They're wearing blue cashmere sweaters over work shirts. And they come in and rather than carry the gun around, they'll leave it behind the bar and ask for it when they come in, or they're going to take it somewhere, then they bring it back and leave it in the bar. And the waitress or the bartender can always claim it's his gun and he has it back there for protection. So this guy, if he's an ex-con, won't be busted on the street for carrying a weapon.

TERKEL: And so we come to the matter of this violence as more and more a part of our society.

THOMPSON: I wouldn't call the Hells Angels the only violent part of our society. I think Lyndon Johnson would be a good Hells Angel. The Angels reflect not only the lower segments of the society but the higher, where violence takes a much more sophisticated and respectable form.

"YOUR WORST FEARS ALWAYS COME TRUE"

INTERVIEW BY HENRY ALLEN
THE WASHINGTON POST BOOK WEEK
JULY 23, 1972

Hunter Thompson, whose new book is called *Fear and Loathing in Las Vegas: A Savage Journey to the Heart of the American Dream*, has this recurring thing which would be a nightmare for anybody else. He says it's real. His wife Sandy backs him up. They are driving out to Dulles Airport, for example. Rush-hour traffic is coiled through the Virginia countryside like a snake that died about two hours ago, just twitching every now and then. Thompson is late (he's always late) for his plane out to cover the California primaries for *Rolling Stone*, the rock newspaper that originally printed *Fear and Loathing*. The traffic jam is pushing him toward teeth-grinding panic. He guns his Volvo down the gravel shoulder, his only clear shot. Then this Rambler pulls out. Not to drive down the shoulder, just far enough to stop Thompson from driving down the shoulder. He knows it's them again; it's happening.

Ordinarily, Hunter Thompson greets the world, even traffic jams, with a poker face, a look of indignant innocence, to be precise, the kind of look that hotel clerks and sky marshals take a professional interest in. But that "who, me?" cool dissolves into a "why me?" anguish when the Rambler with an American flag decal edges onto the shoulder and a kid, wearing a "Try It, You'll Like It" t-shirt, mashes his face insolently against the rear window, looking like somebody committing suicide in a dry cleaner's plastic bag.

"It's been happening all my life," Thompson says in the living room of his rented house off 16th Street. "Goddamn waterheads . . . don't even know me . . . think they're stopping the Nazi invasion . . . I don't know . . . ."

Thompson is talking in these teletype bursts because, among other things, it's Tuesday, and he hasn't slept since Saturday, unless you count the strange Jimson-weed episode on Saturday night when the floors seemed to turn to foam and he spent a few hours in some state other than normal waking consciousness. He's been dosing himself with a hail of Dexedrine tablets to confound the drowsiness, having to finish an article on election-year politics for *Rolling Stone*. The article is five days late; he's always late. The printers have gotten a petition up against him, he says. It keeps happening: decent Americans, like himself, turning on him. He says he isn't paranoid. "There's no such thing as paranoia. The truth is, your worst fears *always* come true."

He screws maybe his seventy-third Marlboro of the day into a cigarette holder and bounds back upstairs in a desperate, duckwalk lope to a room filled with shotguns and the big noise of *Let It Bleed* on the tape recorder. ("If I turn the damn thing off, the walls start closing in on me.") There he types the last paragraphs of his political piece before the printers put a picket line around his house.

"I'm an adrenaline freak," he says. It explains a lot: why he keeps finding himself in one kind of trouble or another; why he elected to spend a year with the subjects of his first book, *Hell's Angels: The Strange and Terrible Saga of the Outlaw Motorcycle Gangs*; and why he wrote *Fear and Loathing*, a chronicle of drug-crazed outrage beyond even the capacity of

Thompson, despite his adrenaline, to express without acceler-
ating into fiction, at least in the best parts.

"Every now and then when your life gets complicated
and the weasels start closing in, the only real cure is to load
up on heinous chemicals and then drive like a bastard from
Hollywood to Las Vegas," he writes in *Fear and Loathing*. This
seems strange, seeing that Las Vegas, as Thompson describes
it in his book, is Mecca for the sort of "weasels" who might
block you from driving down the shoulder of the road, just
on principle. "Pterodactyls lumbering around the corridors
in pools of fresh blood," he calls them, and adds that a Las
Vegas nightclub is "what the whole hep world would be doing
on Saturday night if the Nazis had won the war."

Ostensibly, Thompson, accompanied by his Samoan
attorney, made the trip to the Neon Mecca to write about a
motorcycle race and a district attorney's convention on drugs.
The race and convention, though, rate only passing mention.
Thompson's real subject is outrage. When the weasels start
closing in, outrage is the only way out. *Fear and Loathing* is
part of a continuing literature of outrage that convinces people the world or the author is crazy—or both. J. P. Donleavy,
Terry Southern, Joseph Heller, J. D. Salinger, Tom Wolfe and
all his imitators—all writing astonishingly and outrageously
about outrage and astonishment, the epiphanies coming on
like locomotives, as Snowden's secret in Heller's *Catch-22* or
the gorilla tearing the ship's captain away from the wheel in
Southern's *The Magic Christian*. ("I almost went crazy when
I read that scene," Thompson says.) He was still a "juve-
nile delinquent, very hard case," in Louisville when he read
Donleavy's *The Ginger Man*, whose hero dresses in an ape suit

when his normal effrontery doesn't suffice. "That book made
up my mind that I had to be a writer."

He portrays himself in *Fear and Loathing* as a ravening,
slobbering affront to anything human. But in *Hell's Angels*
he can only come on outrageous, given the subjects, by coming on as clean and reverent as a Dandee Donuts manager.
He's neither. Except for that innocent-as-hell look, he fits
right into his Washington neighborhood, which is shaded
and white, facing Rock Creek Park. He has written about it
as if there were an army of rabid black junkies slouching up
his driveway with brush hooks, "but Hunter tends to make
things worse than they are, sometimes," his wife Sandy says.
She's blonde and thirty-four. She glows with a cheery fatigue.
He is short-haired, big, balding and muscular—six-foot-three
and two hundred pounds. He wears shorts, a sport shirt, and
sneakers.

Thompson is moving back to his home near Aspen (where
he once ran for sheriff in a "freak power" election, and lost)
as soon as possible, breaking the lease on his Juniper Street
house, which involves the usual Hunter Thompson hassle
with the landlord. He won't be taking his pet eight-foot snake
because of another typical Thompson hassle involving a bell-
hop who beat it to death with a vacuum cleaner tube at the
Delmonico Hotel in New York.

"Yeah, I like exotic animals," he says.

What kind of exotic? Exotic like ocelots or exotic like
giant land crabs and Gila monsters?

"Ummmmm, giant land crabs and Gila monsters."

He won't be taking White House press credentials,
either, because the White House never let him in, which "is

like being blackballed at the Playboy Club," he says. But he'll be back in the country where he can "get loaded on mescaline and fire my .44 Magnum out into the dark . . . that long blue flame . . ." (Although, he says he hasn't fired any of his dozen or so weapons in two years).

Besides Sandy, his eight-year-old son Juan, and his shotguns, he'll be taking back a mynah bird which rips the twilight apart with insane laughter and wolf whistles while Thompson stands out front with a big drink in his hand to say goodbye. Also, two big Doberman Pinschers, which, he keeps telling people, are friendly. And, in the garage, his treasure. His wife hates it, he loves it: a life-size, full-color People's Drugstore plastic Christmas-creche choirboy.

"YOU HAD TO GET INTO JOURNALISM JUST TO KEEP UP WITH THE MADNESS"

INTERVIEW BY STUDS TERKEL
THE STUDS TERKEL PROGRAM
MARCH 14, 1973

Excerpts of interview conducted by Studs Terkel of WFMT Radio in Chicago.

STUDS TERKEL: You've written *Fear and Loathing in Las Vegas*, you've run for sheriff of Aspen and almost won. Your thoughts, Hunter Thompson. Six years. Where have we gone?

HUNTER S. THOMPSON: Wow, hmmmmm. A long way. A lot of things have changed in six years. First, that whole era died. What the government wants to call the free-falling era, the sixties, where people really did believe that if you're right, decent, and wore flowers in your hair you'd prevail. But the Angels have now gotten heavily into serious drug sales and Barger just went through one trial for murder and he went through another one.

TERKEL: We should point out Sonny Barger is the head of the Angels.

THOMPSON: Now the Angels are changed. There's no more of that kind of ho-ho thing on the road where you go out and freak the straights. They're too obvious. They're dealing in cars now, they're selling drugs.

•　　•　　•

TERKEL: You covered the last presidential election campaign, that's the basis of your forthcoming book—

THOMPSON: Very much like the Hells Angels.

TERKEL: That's the question I'm asking you.

THOMPSON: Oh, yeah?

TERKEL: Has the Hells Angels approach to life now taken over in a broader way in our society?

THOMPSON: It always was. That's what I was trying to say when I was first in here and I never could quite get it straight— that the Angels themselves weren't important, it was the ethic that they were representing. It was the people with nothing to lose. And you see that in a presidential campaign where it's sort of balls out, and when you lose like George McGovern did, you really lose. It's a power thing where it's all or nothing. You get that with the Angels and you get that with big-time politics, maybe not in local politics.

TERKEL: In *Rolling Stone* there's been this remarkable coverage of yours. Nicholas von Hoffman among others speaks of you as writing the most singular coverage of the 1972 campaign. The phrase we use a lot is "subjective journalism," as opposed to objective. When I say to you, "objective journalism," what's the first thought that comes to mind?

THOMPSON: It's a nice notion. In the current *Columbia*

Journalism Review, on the back page, Wes Gallagher, the president of the AP, says that to say that a journalist can't be objective is like saying a judge can't be fair. But the very argument he makes is belied by the fact that almost no good paper uses the AP anymore except as fillers and emergency stuff.

TERKEL: Has there ever been any such thing as objective journalism?

THOMPSON: It's probably the highest kind of journalism, if you can do it. Nobody that I know has ever done it. And I don't have enough time to learn. I think it'd take about four lifetimes.

TERKEL: You have a perfect case in point in the July 20th *Rolling Stone.* You're in a hotel in New York, and you talk about McGovern and Nixon, and the makers and shakers of the campaign, and the deals and the wheeling. You describe it beautifully. You also speak of your own adventures with a snake. And so did this happen?

THOMPSON: Yeah, the snake was killed at Random House. I've had trouble with them ever since. It's kind of a weird psychological undercurrent in all of our dealings. I got the snake at an alligator farm in Florida. I wanted to wrestle an alligator and the guy said, "No, you can't do that." So I ended up having just to buy a snake, and then he disappeared down a toilet in Florida. I thought he was gone. He came back up the same toilet about four days later while I was in New York. So the people whose toilet he came back up sent it to me. It was a six-foot blue indigo, a very intelligent snake, harmless, totally harmless. They sent it in one of those airline bags and it got out. Some stewardess volunteered to bring it in to Random House. It scared the hell out of them. And so I got in there, I figured well, we'll put a mouse in the box with it and put a big Random House Dictionary on top. Feed the bugger. Leave him here overnight and then I'm going to take him to the hotel. But the mouse figured out what was going to happen to him. It chewed through the cardboard box and the snake went right through the same hole after the mouse.

About dawn the next day the night watchman came out of the white marble stairs at Random House looking across at what was then Cardinal Spellman's headquarters, and saw this horrible six-foot, blue-black serpent coming up the stairs at him. I'm sure he'd never seen any animal bigger than a roach or a rat. He got part of a vacuum cleaner and for about twenty minutes fought this serpent in the lobby.

I'd liked to have seen it. *[Laughs]* He killed it. And then had a nervous breakdown of some kind and was retired. Random House still owes me a good snake.

TERKEL: As a result of which you were not worried about expense accounts because of course at Random House you lost your snake.

THOMPSON: That's right, I ran up about $22,000 on that snake.

TERKEL: The question will come up: did you actually have a snake or is it in your imagination? People ask me this and I say, does it really matter? Don't we live in a surrealistic time?

THOMPSON: We probably do, but I had this snake and every word of that is true.

TERKEL: Oh, you literally had a snake.

THOMPSON: Of course.

TERKEL: I read this as though you'd made it up.

THOMPSON: It would probably be more cheerful for a lot of people if they thought I had made all this stuff up. But no, that's all true.

•   •   •

TERKEL: In the 1968 campaign you found yourself riding in the back of a car with Richard Nixon. Here are you, outrageously dressed by their standards, dangerous in a sense. Can you describe—

THOMPSON: Hostile.

TERKEL: Why don't you set that scene? This is 1968 in New Hampshire. Is that it?

THOMPSON: Yeah. I remember arriving at the Holiday Inn

and seeing Pat Buchanan, who was then doing the at-front muscle work and also speech writing. That was when they were still calling Nixon "The Boss." They still do, in private.

TERKEL: That's the phrase used, "The Boss"?

THOMPSON: Oh yeah, The Boss. And all of his campaign appearances were drills. Like, what's the drill for today? Well, what drill—

TERKEL: Pardon me—

THOMPSON: What drill is The Boss doing today?

TERKEL: Say that slowly again. The word used is a "drill"?

THOMPSON: Drill, right.

TERKEL: A drill, okay.

THOMPSON: If you go somewhere to make a speech or shake hands, you know the boss is doing a drill at 12:30 at the Zing-a-ling diner in Nashua, New Hampshire. So the press would be taken along to watch the boss do his drills. That was the language they used. But when it was over, and after [Republican candidate George] Romney had bombed out, and then [potential candidate Nelson] Rockefeller hadn't come in, it was clear that Nixon was going to win in New Hampshire. I'd been trying, like everybody else, to get a private interview with him for a long time. There was no way, you just couldn't get anywhere near him. They'd hustle him through the lobby every morning at high speed with a big phalanx of people around him.

Finally, I don't know why it happened but Ray Price, the other speechwriter, came up to me and said, "I hate to say this, Hunter, but the boss wants to talk football. I've tried everybody else in the press corps and they don't know football at all. *[Laughs]* And I know you do, but you have to promise not to talk about anything else except football. You can't mention Vietnam, you can't mention people being gassed, you can't mention people being beaten." It was midnight. We're heading back to his Learjet.

TERKEL: This is New Hampshire.

THOMPSON: Yeah, it was right at the end. He was home free. So we had about an hour back from whatever town it was, on the Massachusetts Turnpike. It was about 10-below. And I knew what would happen if I mentioned anything except football. I'd be put out on the damned freeway. So Richard and I sat in the back and talked football, while the cop and Price and Buchanan sat in the front and didn't say a word. But they were waiting, you know. "Any minute this lunatic will say something about Vietnam," and at that point I know that this big yellow Mercury would come to a screeching halt. I'd be put out on the turnpike in the middle of the frozen night.

The odd thing is that I kind of enjoyed it. He really knows football. Nixon is a stone freak for football.

TERKEL: This is the point, perhaps, that things tie together.

With your snake story, someone could say, "Oh, Hunter Thompson made that up." It so happens it is true. Your conversation in the back of the car with the presidential candidate is as surreal as the snake story.

THOMPSON: But it's also just as true.

TERKEL: That's the point.

THOMPSON: Very true.

TERKEL: Isn't this what we're faced with now—that the line blurs, that fantasy and fact become one?

THOMPSON: Somebody said that in an essay in *Partisan Review* or one of those sort of atavistic reviews that reality had become so weird that fiction was no longer plausible. You had to get into journalism just to keep up with the madness.

TERKEL: Yeah.

THOMPSON: Well, I believe that.

●　　　●　　　●

TERKEL: Politics is beyond any drug.

THOMPSON: A four-month mescaline trip, which I never had, thank God, would probably be very exhausting. Well, the campaign was a sixteen-month trip.

TERKEL: So I suppose the word power trip, then, could apply very well.

THOMPSON: You're playing for the highest stakes you can in this country. And you're playing publicly. And every day it changes. It's like a monster game.

TERKEL: This is Hunter S. Thompson I'm talking to. I like the word "doctor." DGS. Doctor of Gonzo Journalism. What is gonzo journalism?

THOMPSON: Oh, boy.

TERKEL: How did the word come about?

THOMPSON: I guess the keywords would be total subjectivity, out-front bias, and—

TERKEL: Out-front bias.

THOMPSON: You have to say what you think. But "participation" is the key word. Where you are a part of the story. You're not covering it, you're not watching it, you get into it. Which was always frustrating to me during the campaign because, playing with that kind of stakes, it's kind of hard to tell [McGovern campaign manager] Frank Mankiewicz that I should be included in the secret meeting to select McGovern's running mate. Although if I had been they'd have been better off. *[Laughs]* Because I was one of the few people to knock [McGovern's first running mate, Thomas] Eagleton.

TERKEL: What you're really saying is that the experts we believe in so much, whether they be in a high office or the big shots, are not really experts at all.

THOMPSON: By the time you get to be an expert you're just an artifact. By the time you're recognized. That that's one of the great troubles I think with the journalists and writers in this country.

TERKEL: Yeah.

THOMPSON: By the time people begin to say, "Oh yes, I know him, he's good," by that time he's raced over the hill, out of his head, writing gibberish and repeating himself.

•   •   •

THOMPSON: What politics in this country has become is a mockery, just a bad joke. When you look back at the Bill of Rights and the Declaration of Independence, we've become a mockery of ourselves. The energy that's out there to change the system in this country is almost immeasurable.

TERKEL: Yeah. Perhaps this—

THOMPSON: It's frightening and it's also—

TERKEL: Your point is it could go either way depending upon the people. It could go either way.

THOMPSON: I think people are just tired of this same old tripe.

TERKEL: The energy is there. We're told a lot about apathy, but you're saying there's tremendous energy underneath. Depends on which way it's channeled.

THOMPSON: If you're told you have a duty to buy a car tomorrow, but it has to be either a Ford or a Chevy, then that would get me pretty apathetic. I'd say the hell with it. What we need is something else.

TERKEL: We're talking about the question of choice.

THOMPSON: The system precludes that, in a sense.

TERKEL: Yeah.

THOMPSON: I think the next big-time national politician who comes along and runs on a realistic platform to really shake the system will cause a lot of trouble. He might not win, but he will have a veto power over whoever does win.

POLITICAL HIGHS AND LOWS

INTERVIEW BY JANE PERLEZ
WASHINGTON JOURNALISM REVIEW
NOVEMBER / DECEMBER 1979

This interview was done in September 1979, a few months before the 1980 primaries began. Jimmy Carter was regarded as vulnerable, weakened by rampant inflation and a widespread sense that he couldn't handle the presidency. Ted Kennedy was expected to seize the moment and run to Carter's left, which in November he did. It's revealing that the Republican candidates are never even mentioned in the following conversation, even though one of them—Ronald Reagan—eventually beat Carter in the general election, ushering in a new era.

JANE PERLEZ: I thought I'd start by asking where you've been. You told Ron Rosenbaum of *High Times* magazine two years ago that you'd get back into politics when you found it necessary, but that there were better things to do, like buying an opium den in Singapore or a whorehouse in Maine. You haven't done either of those two things.

HUNTER S. THOMPSON: No, Hollywood has taken care of that for me. I didn't realize you could also go to Hollywood. So I've been out there playing around for about a year. It's interesting to see what you can do there. I want to see if I want to stay with it or not. Seems that it could be fun to do. But on the other hand it's so different—you have to work with so many people and the politics are so weird, I'm not sure I could handle it. Then you figure, what the hell. There's a lot of money out of it.

PERLEZ: More money than an advance for a campaign book?

THOMPSON: Another campaign book would be impossible. I don't see any point in doing that either. That would be backsliding.

PERLEZ: Do you think that it is impossible for you, or do you think campaign books per se are a thing of the past?

THOMPSON: No, somebody should do it. But not me. You can sort of sneak up on [a campaign] like Teddy White [author of *The Making of the President*] in 1960. Then they know what you're doing. Then either you become absorbed into it, you become a part of it, or else they get hostile. Or both. In my case, some people got hostile, and some people tried to absorb me.

Then when you go back to write another book, they're watching for you. The first time is nice, because they really don't know what you're doing at all. But once they know, you become trapped into playing the game—you, the book writer, the chronicler—and they treat you like that. You get invited to things that you would have been put out of before, and they know, for one thing, that the book doesn't come out until the campaign is over. So if you're writing a book, in theory, you have a lot more access than somebody who is writing for next week or tomorrow. There are a lot of crimes people will admit to later on, but not during the campaign.

PERLEZ: How much of the 1976 campaign did you cover? And why did you give it up?

THOMPSON: I got through the Florida primary. I knew right away I wouldn't be able to make it all the way through. I was looking for enough so I could do one piece and then get out. The Florida primary seemed to me where Carter was clearly off and running. So I quit. Then by the time I wrote the thing, it was almost convention time.

PERLEZ: In the decision to get out, how important was the fact that you felt crippled by knowing too much which you couldn't write?

THOMPSON: That's very inhibiting, something I'd rather not have to cope with again. It sneaks up on you, so that all of a sudden you know too much. It isn't as though they decided to give you the choice, do you want to know too much? And then you decided. All of a sudden you realize, "Ye gods, what am I doing here?" You've got two options. You can remind them by writing something, or you can step all over them. Depends whether you like them or not. That's what it all comes down to, whether you like them.

PERLEZ: Did you find that you liked the Carter people too much?

THOMPSON: They were the loosest. Like the McGovern campaign in 1972. Right away you find out where the fun is, where the dope is. People really try and enjoy campaigns. When you find the campaign so dreary, and then you find people you really like to be around—it hardly matters whether you like their politics. It gets so god-awful dreary, that anyone who can make you laugh is welcome.

PERLEZ: You seem to have no doubt that Kennedy will succeed.

THOMPSON: I'd be surprised if Carter survived the first three primaries.

PERLEZ: But you were one of the first to tell us that he was a zealot and no one should underestimate his tenacity.

THOMPSON: Well, tenacity is one thing, but what I didn't realize is that he was incompetent. I'm surprised that he conned me on that point real badly. I have some tapes of him telling me—it's very sad, it sounded like a high school civics major telling you how he's going to run the country.

I've got eight hours of tape of him in '74, talking about worms in the ground and how the grass grows, driving around with him in a thunderstorm . . . I might even believe it again. Listening to the tapes, he sounds like a different person, the voice is different, he seems twenty years younger. I just thought it would be nice not to have to fight the White House for a while and have somebody mind the store. After ten years of being gassed and all that shit, I was just tired of it. And then the choice comes down to Humphrey, Ford, or Carter, then you can't hesitate too long. But he just proved to be an incompetent. He just can't do it.

PERLEZ: Can you delineate the incompetence?

THOMPSON: It would be hard to separate the incompetence from everything else he does because they seem to be intertwined.

PERLEZ: Do you think it's the people around him?

THOMPSON: Oh yeah, that's part of it.

PERLEZ: [Jody] Powell and [Hamilton] Jordan and [Tim] Kraft, [all advisers and aides]?

THOMPSON: Yeah, mainly that his advice comes always from the same people. They began paranoid, and now they're real paranoid. So when you get your advice from all those people, all the time, you get like Nixon. It's the bunker mentality. He doesn't trust people enough to consult people outside his inner circle.

PERLEZ: How do you perceive Kennedy?

THOMPSON: I think he's a very able and effective senator. In terms of who's competent and who's not, Kennedy is demonstrably more so than Carter. Just as a general rule, Teddy has always had, I'd say, the best staff in Washington. To travel with Kennedy is almost like traveling with a very polished presidential campaign, even though he's a senator going to make a weekend speech.

PERLEZ: Are they fun to be with?

THOMPSON: The candidates are never fun to be with. The Kennedy people are all business. There wouldn't be much hanging out, getting stoned at night.

PERLEZ: Looking back on it, don't you think the Carter staff were somewhat naïve?

THOMPSON: Yes, very. I think they thought that once they go into the White House they'd be immune, like Nixon, or like Nixon thought. I think once you win, you think, we got past that. They didn't seem to learn much, once they got into the White House. They acted as though they were still running a campaign out of Georgia. As it turns out, getting elected president is pretty easy. It's being president that's tough.

PERLEZ: How much do you think the clubbiness between the blue-chip reporters and the blue-chip assistants helped Carter get the coverage he wanted?

THOMPSON: A tremendous amount. It gave Carter credibility. Once you're sympathetic to a candidate, it's easy to see why he might be better.

PERLEZ: In the fifties and sixties, it used to be drinking. What's new, I suppose, is that it's [political aides] doing dope and coke.

THOMPSON: Don't ever forget sex in there. That would be a nasty can of worms to open. Well, the coke ain't so bad, but man the sex, oh, oh! Let me tell you about that. You could drop a few things that would make Chappaquiddick seem too boring to talk about.*

PERLEZ: If you were going to cover this campaign, what angle would you take, how would you go about it?

THOMPSON: You'd have to say what I was working for.

PERLEZ: Let's start with a daily newspaper.

THOMPSON: You don't have much choice in those situations. The more often you have to publish, the more you're locked into the routine of the campaign.

PERLEZ: Let's talk about pieces for, say, *Esquire*, which might be put into a book.

THOMPSON: That's an odd area, where you're writing stuff that appears during the campaign and you might also be writing a book, then people really don't know what you're going to do. Like Teddy White. He gets so much more access because he's not writing during the campaign. I'd go into this to write a book. First of all, there's a lot more money in a book. I thought about that last time. I wasn't going to write during the campaign. I was going to write a book.

PERLEZ: But how would you approach the book?

---

*Incident in 1969 when Ted Kennedy drove off a bridge, killing Mary Jo Kopechne, a young campaign worker.

THOMPSON: It all depends; you never know what's going to happen in a campaign. A campaign develops its own personality as it goes along, unless it's like a Nixon-Kennedy campaign, then you know ahead of time.

PERLEZ: Let's talk about the newspaper reporters. You've talked about the invidious situation that the reporters get into by knowing their sources so well, that they don't want to hurt them because they want to keep access. How do you get over that double bind?

THOMPSON: I don't know. First of all, you have to make sure you don't value friends in Washington. You should not live in Washington. If you live and work in Washington there's no way you can get over it. Sooner or later you're going to want something and they'll say, "You son of a bitch, remember that thing you wrote back in March?" which gives them an excuse forever not to talk to you. So you really have to make your choice early. It works out if you make the right choice and humor the right people.

PERLEZ: Things don't seem to change much. Already in New Hampshire there are reporters who've been covering campaigns for the last three or four times.

THOMPSON: Five or six times for some. For a while there seemed to be a new kind of reporter covering campaigns. But they didn't appear much in '76. I don't know exactly what happened. I thought Timothy Crouse [author of *The Boys on* *the Bus*, a behind-the-scenes account] and I cut out in a whole new direction with the books we did in '72. But no one really picked that up.

PERLEZ: You think Carter might take a vacation for four years?

THOMPSON: That'd be nice. He'd learn something about the economy and come back in four years and there might be this great reservoir of good feeling for this person who'd admitted he couldn't handle it. That might be a good calculated risk. Nobody tried that before. Teddy Roosevelt, maybe. It would be a ballsy move to decide that you needed a little bit more study and to promise to run again in 1984. And actually to plan for it. Campaign all around the goddamn world. I don't know who'd pay for that. It would be a real trip if he did that. People would be impressed.

PERLEZ: He's always prided himself on ballsy moves, like Cabinet shake-ups.

THOMPSON: He has to have a little more intelligence to know that that's not enough and that you've got to have something more. Anyone can be ballsy. It's trying to make it work that's hard.

PERLEZ: Let's talk about writing. You've said that Gonzo journalism is, in a way, simply first-draft journalism. If you'd done second drafts, how would they have been different?

THOMPSON: Quieter. I very rarely add crazier things in a second draft.

PERLEZ: What have you done second drafts on?

THOMPSON: It's been a long time.

PERLEZ: The *National Observer* pieces [written in the early 1960s]?

THOMPSON: There may have been two drafts. The Vegas book was the last time I did a second, third, sometimes fourth draft.

PERLEZ: The Vegas book? Seems that's the book everyone perceived as being the most undrafted.

THOMPSON: That's why I liked the book. It's finely crafted in the way it's put together. There are only about fifteen words in there that shouldn't be. I like that. Drafting is a very fine tool. I miss that. It usually makes it better, though you can worry a piece to death. It gives me a chance to get out the craziness of the night before. I figure the night before, I can write it up, write anything, then the next day when I come back and look at it, I knock out the parts that are too crazy.

PERLEZ: It's interesting that the new piece by Norman Mailer in *Playboy* on [convicted killer] Gary Gilmore is back to basics, and straight reporting. Have you read it?

THOMPSON: No, but I heard that. Kind of flat, it sounded good.

PERLEZ: Do you see that as a trend? Perhaps the interjection of the reporter in stories has run its phase?

THOMPSON: I don't see any real reason for it, either way. I think in Mailer's case and in mine, you get tired of doing the same thing after a while.

PERLEZ: Isn't it a tremendous effort to keep yourself involved in the piece?

THOMPSON: I don't find that so much. It's just all first draft stuff. [*The Great Shark Hunt*] is a collection of first drafts. I haven't changed anything since I put them in *Rolling Stone*, except for typos. It would all be about half as personalized as it is if I had the time to do a second draft.

I finished that one thing, being a Gonzo journalist—it was fun but it gets real old. I was a straight journalist for a while. So maybe what Norman is doing . . . maybe back to straight reporting.

If Mailer had time to do a second draft, or I had, neither one of our styles would be what they are now. I think what it comes from is trying to do too much on a deadline that didn't allow for it. What it does is produce this crazy, frantic tone to it that if you don't do a second draft, it comes through in the writing. People call it Gonzo journalism, but it's carelessness, that's what it is.

PERLEZ: Born out of the situation?

THOMPSON: Yeah, it's unavoidable. If I'd had more time, I'd probably have cured myself. I don't know what that would have done for it or me.

But when you get on deadlines you can't get back to it the next afternoon. It has to go off. You pull it out of the typewriter, put it over the mojo wire and bang, it's gone. I've even stopped editing pages, much less the writing. Put it in the typewriter and don't even bother to correct the typos. Try to call it in. Very slowly I'm getting around the typewriter and the printing pages. I believe sometime soon I'll be able to take it straight from babbling gibberish to some kind of photo display. I was one of the first journalists to use a tape recorder.

PERLEZ: When?

THOMPSON: The *Hell's Angels* book. That was the first time they had cassette recorders. Before that you had to use the reel-to-reel stuff. But once they got it down to that size, I saw a whole new world beckoning.

PERLEZ: The Hells Angels guys weren't intimidated by it?

THOMPSON: They didn't see it. They saw the reel-to-reel stuff earlier and threatened to kill me. But this, I just wore in a shoulder holster, all of a sudden you don't have to write notes anymore. The worst thing about tape is listening to it.

PERLEZ: How do you manage that?

THOMPSON: I appreciate the remote pause. I try to be real conscious when I'm taping something that I'll have to listen to it, so I use the remote pause so that if you have five minutes of the waiter coming into the room, then I can just cut it off. Listening to four hours of tape after listening to a candidate can be real interesting for one day, but boy if you have to do it constantly, it can drive you mad. Most things you hear, they don't make any sense anyway. You have to separate the wheat from the chaff, and the more you have, the harder it is to do it. So what you end up doing is trying to edit on the spot. I used to put my mic in my watchband, down my sleeve, so that you'd pick it up. When you put your hand in your pocket you're in trouble.

PERLEZ: When you're listening to the stuff at night, how do you get from the spoken word onto the typewriter?

THOMPSON: I usually go back over it and listen and write down the things that I like exactly as I heard them. You get to listen to it, write it down in legal pads, then you go over it and get totally accurate quotes. You'd be amazed how just about impossible— if you're going to listen to somebody in a volatile situation—to get, say, a five-minute, even a two-minute, quote right. From a tape recorder you can get all kinds of asides. If you tape it right and write down exactly what was said, it makes a big difference.

PERLEZ: Do you think you could have written anything after *Hell's Angels* without a tape recorder?

THOMPSON: It would have been different. Because I saw what the tape recorder could do. I could just drive around in the car and keep the tape recorder out on the seat and you'd hear all of a sudden some horrible ripping sound, a fence being torn down, and you hear screams. There's no amount of memory that can bring it back to you that perfectly—that you can hear the sound of a fence being ripped out of the ground and hear what it sounds like. What I do is tape it on the smallest unit, but when I play it back—I have eighty speakers in my living room so when I play it back I pick up everything. It's like being in the scene. There's no way that notes can bring that back to you. I have twenty speakers in every corner, so I can just sit in the middle.

PERLEZ: So there is a reason why you go back to Colorado, aside from the mountains and the clean air. It's to be near your equipment.

THOMPSON: I've got so much equipment now I can't carry it around anymore. I used to be able to carry it with me.

PERLEZ: Do you see Bill Cardozo [*The Boston Globe* editor who first called Thompson a Gonzo journalist]?

THOMPSON: He's out in San Francisco writing a book on some murder in Palm Springs. Some freak up in Boston invented the term, some eighth generation of street kid, but it was Cardozo who tied it to journalism. I thought, "That's a good word. I'll be one of those." It worked.

THE DOCTOR IS IN

INTERVIEW BY CURTIS WILKIE
THE BOSTON GLOBE MAGAZINE
JANUARY 7, 1988

FEAR AND LOATHING AT WOODY CREEK ... NOTES FROM A STRANGE TIME ... A NEW "GENERATION OF SWINE" ... GONZO MAN JOINS JINGO PAPER

> "I'm older now, but still running against the wind."
> —Bob Seger, *"Against the Wind"*

So many of the icons of our generation are in ruins, victims of time and Reagan's cultural revolution. "Just say no" are the new catchwords, and the Red Queen and White Rabbit have been replaced by King Condom. John Lennon is seven years dead, and Timothy Leary might as well be. Jerry Rubin promotes capitalism. Janis and Jimi, Duane Allman, and Jim Morrison are gone. Otis Redding and Mama Cass, gone. All gone. James Brown's screams have lost their pitch. Lynyrd Skynyrd's "Free Bird" crashed in a swamp. Richard Brautigan snuffed himself. The landscape is littered with burned-out cases, children of the 1950s who spent themselves over the next two decades like Roman candles.

But there is a survivor, unrepentant and unforgiving, lurking in a log cabin high in the Colorado Rockies. Hunter S. Thompson just reached the landmark age of fifty, and after a midlife lull when it was feared he was finished, the outlaw prince of Gonzo journalism is writing again with the fury of a shark in a feeding frenzy. As one of the last two-fisted drinkers, Thompson defies the legacy of Dylan Thomas, who died before forty of what the coroner called "insult to the brain." Despite years of physical abuse—best characterized by an orgy of drugs and alcohol at a law-enforcement convention he chronicled in *Fear and Loathing in Las Vegas* in the early 1970s—Thompson, amazingly, still looks healthy enough to challenge a professional athlete.

Searching through my beer-sodden notes after several days in his company on the fringes of Aspen in December, I find one of his quotes: "It only feels like one long year since I was twenty-two. I never grew up." Exactly. After a half-century, Hunter Thompson is a macho Peter Pan.

His political writing, which appears in a syndicated weekly column in the *San Francisco Examiner,* has regained the intensity of his work in *Rolling Stone* magazine nearly twenty years ago, when he was heaping scorn on Richard M. Nixon, Hubert H. Humphrey, and other officials. His chief target these days is the right-wing gang in the Republican Party. If Thompson can get his act together—and his book editor was threatening to abort the project when I was in Aspen unless he met a deadline—a collection of his recent columns will be published this year by Summit Books under the title *Generation of Swine.*

Just as he described Humphrey in 1972 as "a treacherous, gutless old ward-heeler who should be put in a goddamn bottle and sent out with the Japanese Current," Thompson is now relentlessly keelhauling another vice president, George Bush. Of Bush, Thompson wrote in a recent column, "He has the instincts of a dung beetle. No living politician can match his talent for soiling himself in public. Bush will seek out filth wherever it lives—going without sleep for days at a time if necessary—and when he finds a new heap he will fall down and wallow crazily in it, making snorting sounds out of his nose and rolling over on his back and kicking his legs up in the air like a wild hog coming to water."

Why am I repeating these things? It is all madness, these irresponsible descriptions and apocryphal stories: Gonzo journalism run amok. Yet underneath the lurid gibberish it is possible to sniff out, like truffles, kernels of wisdom and truth. Thompson describes Gonzo journalism—his term for his work—as "a style of reporting based on William Faulkner's idea that the best fiction is far more true than any kind of journalism."

He sprung on the world this novel approach to political journalism during the 1972 presidential campaign, as he followed Edmund S. Muskie's breakdown in the primaries, a collapse accompanied by the candidate's public tears in New Hampshire and private fits of rage. In his reports to *Rolling Stone*, which resulted in the book *Fear and Loathing on the Campaign Trail '72*, Thompson speculated that Muskie's reactions were caused by injections of the jungle drug Ibogaine, which left his "brain almost paralyzed by hallucinations at the time; he looked out at that crowd and saw Gila monsters instead of people . . ."

This year, Thompson has a new mandate to skewer the latest generation of politicians, and his pulpit, of all places, is that flagship of the Hearst empire, the *San Francisco Examiner*, a newspaper he once described as "particularly influential among those who fear King George III might still be alive in Argentina." Under the leadership of William Randolph Hearst III, the paper has hired Thompson and, among others, another sixties renegade, Warren Hinckle, in an effort to jazz up its traditionally conservative image.

The arrangement permits Thompson to write from his

own lair, a cabin at Woody Creek, about ten miles outside Aspen. "I'm a hillbilly," he says, "a lazy bastard." Late
one night, while Thompson and I were talking in the clut-
tered kitchen of his home—the erstwhile "National Affairs
Desk" of *Rolling Stone*—Will Hearst telephoned to inquire
about the whereabouts of an overdue column. Thompson
put me on the line and disappeared. An awkward conversation ensued. I observed that the *Examiner* seemed a strange
outlet for Hunter Thompson. Hearst replied that publishing
Thompson was in the "libertarian" tradition of a newspaper
chain that once carried iconoclasts such as Mark Twain and
Ambrose Bierce. "It is slow getting copy out of him," Will
Hearst admitted. Thompson had still not reappeared. "Tell
him we demand his copy tonight," Hearst said. "He has got
to call back in two hours."

Under pressure, and using an old-fashioned typewriter,
Thompson cobbled together two thoughts he had already put
down on tattered paper. As the supply of Molson dwindled
in an auxiliary beer refrigerator outside the kitchen where he
writes, Hunter Thompson met another deadline.

THE DOCTOR IS IN . . . BRAINRAPERS AND GREEDHEADS . . . REAGAN ON THE GIBBET . . . THE SECRET SERVICE IS WATCHING . . .

"Whether he is writing the exact truth—or has raised it a few
notches to make a point about hypocrisy and greed in modern America—is not the point. The point is he is writing well,
and with humor, an acid-head Mencken reincarnated . . ."
                                    —William Zinsser, *On Writing Well*

In person, Thompson is as wild and undisciplined, entertaining and irreverent, as his writing. If he sleeps, it is like a vampire—by day. An avowed speed freak, he can go for days without rest. The night does not belong to Michelob; it belongs to Hunter Stockton Thompson. Dr. Thompson, if you will. He insists upon the title, saying that he is a doctor of "philosophy, chemotherapy and divinity."

He is from Louisville, Kentucky, but vague about his educational background, mumbling something about attending Columbia University and other institutions of higher learning. In a piece on "The Nonstudent Left" he wrote for *The Nation* in 1965, Thompson said, "In 1958, I drifted north from Kentucky and became a nonstudent at Columbia. I signed up for two courses and am still getting bills for the tuition." No matter. How many prophets do you know with a college education?

For a while, he toiled as a straight journalist. As a young man, he applied for a job on the *San Juan Star* in Puerto Rico, but the managing editor, a fellow named William Kennedy, turned him down. (All is forgiven. Thompson hopes Kennedy, who became a prize-winning novelist in Albany, New York, will write an introduction for *Generation of Swine*.) Thompson's first job in journalism was at *Time* magazine. He was a copy boy. He later wrote for a daily newspaper in Middletown, New York, but was fired after attacking a vending machine with a hammer. He finally gained employment at a respectable weekly newspaper, the *National Observer*, but it went out of business. At the time, he was reporting the news conventionally. All that would change.

Living in California's Big Sur country, he wrote a book,

Hell's Angels, which culminated with his own stomping by the motorcycle gang. But the real catharsis would come in Chicago, just as it did for so many of his contemporaries. In an essay about the episode that turned an age of idealists into cynics, Thompson wrote:

"Probably it was Chicago—that brainraping week in August of '68. I went to the Democratic convention as a journalist, and returned a raving beast. For me, that week in Chicago was far worse than the worst bad acid trip I'd even heard rumors about. It permanently altered my brain chemistry, and my first new idea—when I finally calmed down—was an absolute conviction there was no possibility for any personal truce, for me, in a nation that could hatch and be proud of a malignant monster like Chicago."

He moved to Aspen and helped lead an insurgent political movement against "a mean bunch of rednecks" who ruled the county. The "Freak Power" ticket had its headquarters in the bar of the Hotel Jerome, a gathering spot at the time for "freaks, heads, fun-hogs, and weird night-people of every description." Thompson ran for sheriff in 1970, mocking the law-and-order crowd by shaving his head and wearing sinister sunglasses in campaign posters. His platform called for ripping the streets with jackhammers and planting sod in place of asphalt, renaming Aspen "Fat City" in order to "prevent greedheads, land-rapers, and other human jackals from capitalizing" on the town's name, and installing a "bastinado platform and a set of stocks" on the courthouse lawn to punish drug dealers who cheated customers.

He lost, but the political complexion of Aspen was changed irrevocably. Today the little town, with a population of 8,000 people and an altitude of 8,000 feet, is both precious and radicalized. It serves as the winter home of Jack Nicholson, Goldie Hawn, and other celebrities, as well as hundreds of sybaritic visitors. Aspen's streets are lined with chic boutiques and bars with names like The Red Onion.

The town has become so trendy that Thompson rarely goes beyond the Woody Creek Tavern, a rustic watering spot located a couple of switchbacks down the mountain from Owl Farm, where he lives. Cigarette smoke hangs low in the tavern, where cowboys and construction workers wear ragged sheepskin jackets, denims and frayed ten-gallon hats. The food is cheap but sustaining, and the jukebox does not carry Barry Manilow. Jill, the cook, points out that it may be the only bar in the world without a mirror. The clientele at the Woody Creek Tavern is not narcissistic.

One night we met there for dinner, and Thompson burst through the door carrying a hideous, rubber facsimile of a sickly grinning Ronald Reagan he had bought at an airport. The cowboys cheered, but one table was occupied by stylishly dressed après-skiers who had apparently decided to visit this "quaint little place" for dinner. The tourists watched in horror as Thompson puffed the Reagan device to life-size. He cursed loudly after discovering it was not the sort of steel-based toy he could use as a punching bag. A cry of "String him up!" arose from the bar. Thompson and Gaylord Guenin, the major-domo of Woody Creek Tavern, disappeared into the attic and returned with a coil of rope. As he worked on a goblet of Chivas Regal and a Molson on the side, Thompson constructed a hangman's noose, fitted it over the rubberized neck, and left the ersatz president dangling in effigy from a rafter. "I always thought he was an elderly dingbat," he declared, "a silly old fool."

The Secret Service would not have been amused. The agency's travails with Thompson date back to the time in Florida in 1972 when he loaned his press credentials during a Muskie whistle-stop trip to "The Boohoo," a bartender-desperado named Peter Sheridan who would eventually kill himself in a motorcycle wreck. While Muskie, then an august senator and the leading candidate for the Democratic nomination, attempted to deliver a speech from the caboose at the Miami train station, "The Boohoo" used his place in the press area to claw at Muskie's pants, demanding more gin.

This past year, Thompson says, the Secret Service has investigated his vicious comments about George Bush, whom Thompson claims is "doomed." As the Iran-Contra affair unfolded, Thompson wrote that the "hallways in the White House basement were slick with human scum. Even the Gipper was bleeding and George Bush was walking around like a man with both wrists slit and trying to ignore the blood." Blaming Bush for the contra connection, Thompson continued his screed: "Before this thing is over, George will know agonies far worse than simple gout, or leech fever, or even the heartbreak of psoriasis. There is already talk among his neighbors up there in Kennebunkport about strapping him onto one of those old-timey dunking stools and letting the local boys have a go at him."

In a subsequent column, he depicted a scene in which Bush learns he is linked to Lieutenant Colonel Oliver North, a man Thompson described as "the Charles Manson figure in this hideous scandal that crawls like a plague of maggots. . ."

At a White House meeting, Thompson reported, "George went stiff, then dropped to his knees like a wino and wept openly in front of his staff people. . . The shrewd and treacherous vice president was no longer clean."

Thompson prides himself on his own "outlaw" status. Last year, golfing with his friend Ed Bradley of *60 Minutes*, he was charged with firing a shotgun on the Aspen municipal course. My sources say he fired two "warning shots" near a man on a lawn-mower tractor who was disrupting their game. Thompson showed me how he stuffs the shotgun, like a 3-wood, into his golf bag for "protection." He insisted he simply shot it once into the air for fun. Bradley testified he heard a mysterious shot, but saw nothing. Thompson was fined $100.

There is a pickle jar on the shelf of the Woody Creek Tavern devoted to the "Hunter S. Thompson Defense Fund." A sign on the jar says, "Help Save This Pathetic Victim of Police Brutality. FREE THE DOCTOR." Contributions have included small change, dollar bills, condoms, a piece of beef jerky, and some hamster droppings.

FLIGHT TO THE UNKNOWN . . . THE PHOENIX ALSO RISES . . . REMEMBRANCE OF THINGS PAST . . . REVENGE IN ORLANDO . . .

"O lost, and by the wind grieved, ghost, come back again."
—Thomas Wolfe, *Look Homeward, Angel*

The inspiration to track down Thompson came after a Boston cabdriver, who admired his reporting, asked me what ever happened to the wizard of Gonzo journalism. After falling out with Jann Wenner, the editor and publisher of *Rolling Stone*, Thompson seemed to have disappeared from the scene. But I knew he was now writing a column for the *Examiner*, and after placing calls to his answering service, his editor, and the Woody Creek Tavern, I got a collect call late one night from "Dr. Thompson."

We agreed to meet in Aspen in early December. He urged me not to fly Continental Airlines, which had just suffered a crash in the snow at Denver that cost a number of lives. In that week's column, Thompson savaged Continental for earning "what is beginning to look like the ugliest reputation in the American business community since the Edsel, thalidomide, or the economic wisdom of Herbert Hoover." So I took United. En route to Denver, rereading *The Great Shark Hunt*, an anthology of Thompson's work, I came across this paragraph from 1970: "Flying United, to me, is like crossing the Andes in a prison bus. There is no question in my mind that somebody like Pat Nixon personally approves every United stewardess. Nowhere in the Western world is there anything to equal the collection of self-righteous shrews who staff the 'friendly skies' of United."

By the time I got to Aspen, the author had vanished. At the Woody Creek Tavern there were reports of a "sighting" in Phoenix. The next day, Thompson called the Hotel Jerome to assure me he was on his way home after dealing with an "emergency." He related a strange tale of how his travels had been diverted to Phoenix in order for him to see Maria—who may or may not be his wife. After returning to Colorado, he showed me her photograph. She is young and lovely and, according to Thompson, the daughter of a wealthy Pakistani who is not amused by their relationship. The father, he swears, put out a contract on his life. "When we met, he asked me, 'Just what kind of doctor are you?' He didn't have the vaguest idea who I was. Now he knows. It gets me in a lot of trouble." Thompson's voice trailed off, "If my daughter ran off with a freak when she was twenty-two . . ."

I first encountered Hunter Thompson during the McGovern campaign in 1972. We met one night covering the Ohio primary. J. Edgar Hoover had just died, and we celebrated the end of his despotic rule of the FBI through a long night's journey into morning, while corrupt politicians delayed the count of the primary vote in an attempt to steal the election for Humphrey.

I was witness to Thompson's aberrant behavior later that year as a trainload of journalists followed George McGovern through the San Joaquin Valley during the California primary. A European camera crew had been particularly obnoxious, pushing and shoving us to obtain a better angle. Thompson produced a hunting knife and threatened to cut the cord that bound the soundman to the cameraman—indeed, to relieve them of certain vital organs if they did not desist. They fled in terror.

Four years later, we were having dinner at the Sheraton Wayfarer near Manchester as the New Hampshire primary approached. The management had informed Thompson there was no room for him at the inn. He was seething because he felt he had helped immortalize the hotel in his book about the last campaign. He took matters into his own hands, literally. Grabbing a fork, he marched to the desk and vowed to gouge out the eardrum of the night clerk. A room was found for him.

Thompson was partially responsible for the rise of Jimmy Carter that year, "turning on" the readers of *Rolling Stone* to this obscure governor of Georgia. He lavishly praised a Law Day speech Carter had delivered in 1974, a performance Thompson ranked with General Douglas MacArthur's "old soldiers never die" address to Congress as a Great American Speech. Carter was grateful, and over the course of the early 1976 campaign, Thompson felt he had a special franchise with the candidate. He expected an interview with Carter as they flew from Orlando to Chicago on the morning after Carter's triumph in the Florida primary, but Carter stiffed him. The future Democratic nominee said he was too tired and wanted to sleep. Muttering and glowering upon arrival at O'Hare Airport, Thompson caught the next plane back to Orlando to besiege the hotel room where Hamilton Jordan—Carter's campaign manager—was still sleeping. When Jordan refused to respond to Thompson's screeching, the national affairs correspondent for *Rolling Stone* soaked the base of Jordan's door with lighter fluid and set it ablaze.

Over the course of his career, Thompson has pillaged many hotels. One correspondent who attended the cataclysmic events in Vietnam in 1975 remembers that the sound of Thompson crashing down the steps of Saigon's Continental Hotel was louder than the artillery of the approaching North Vietnamese Army.

THE DUKE OF *DOONESBURY*... BIMBOS AND BOMB-SHELLS... GIVING ODDS IN AN ODD TIME... THE DOCTOR OF PHILOSOPHY...

"By sundown on Friday the banshee had screamed for more stiffs than the morgues could hold, and the jails were filling up like cheap hotels in Calcutta."

—Hunter S. Thompson, *San Francisco Examiner*

Thompson has been cultivating an outlandish persona for years—the drunken, raving, dope fiend who narrated *Fear and Loathing in Las Vegas*. The book first appeared in *Rolling Stone* and was allegedly written by "Raoul Duke," a pseudonym that Thompson says he picked "off the wall." Raoul Duke is still listed as "Contributing Editor (Sports)" on the *Rolling Stone* masthead. Thompson, for that matter, has the title of "Health & Fitness Editor" for a publication named *Bathroom Journal*. Duke, of course, was transmogrified by Garry Trudeau into a durable cartoon-strip character in *Doonesbury*. Trudeau's Duke resembles Thompson: the balding head, the sunglasses, the cigarette holder, the reckless talk of drug deals and scams. Oddly enough, Thompson and Trudeau, the two high priests of American satire who both harass Bush unmercifully, have never met. It is just as well.

After Duke first appeared in the cartoon more than a decade ago, Thompson sent Trudeau several menacing letters in which the subject of the artist's dismemberment was raised. At the time, Thompson's marriage to his first wife, Sandy, was crumbling, and he resented the inclusion of her name in the comic strip. Thompson says he no longer looks at

Doonesbury, where Duke has degenerated to zombie status.

Even today, Thompson will not discuss his divorce. He gestured as if to slit my throat, brandishing a steak knife from the Woody Creek Tavern, if I brought it up. But he is proud of a product of that union, his twenty-two-year-old son Juan, a student at the University of Colorado.

There may not be a sober side to Hunter Thompson, but there is a generous one. It turns out that one of his running mates is Semmes Luckett, who was my college roommate in 1959. Like half of the residents of Aspen, it seems, Luckett got turned in to the Feds by an informer a few years ago. He copped a plea for moving massive shipments of what he calls "herbs," did some time in a halfway house, and is now in the midst of a five-year probation period. Things have not always been easy for him, but when he was down-and-out, he says, Thompson sent him a large, unsolicited check.

While I was in Aspen, another of Thompson's friends was badly hurt in a car wreck. He immediately began making arrangements to take care of the victim's sixteen-year-old son.

And for all of the nihilistic language he uses, Thompson cares about the American political process. When he accepts speaking engagements on campuses, he says, "I preach to the college students that politics is the art to control your environment. . . . In a democracy, you've got to believe you can make a difference."

His problem is that he distrusts most of the politicians involved. We didn't know it the last night we talked politics, but Gary Hart would be back in the race the next day.*

---

*Hart had dropped out of the race for the Democratic nomination after reporters found him canoodling with a woman, Donna Rice.

Even though Hart was supposedly gone at that moment, he was not forgotten. In fact, he was the butt of much derision, even though Thompson and Hart are old Colorado friends. (I remember Thompson arriving at a low moment during the Hart effort in 1984 with heavy-duty cables to "jump-start" the campaign.) There is a bogus letter signed "Gary," written on US Senate stationery, that adorns one wall of the Woody Creek Tavern. Written in a style suspiciously similar to Thompson's prose, the letter refers to the Donna Rice affair and concludes, "Thank God I got rid of her before she got her rotten little teeth into me."

Thompson says that as a reporter, he would never stake out a candidate's home "unless he was suspected of selling cocaine to little children. There we might draw the line. We all know these candidates are womanizers. Sex never hurt anybody. In the meantime we lose track of what matters. The press becomes obsessed with the *National Enquirer* syndrome. There are more ominous things happening in politics than a bimbo from Miami. They've been around all the time."

Thompson predicts Sen. Edward M. Kennedy will get into the race and hopes he will win the presidency this year, though he adds, "I like Gary Hart better than Kennedy." Thompson is not bothered by what tarnishes both men. "So Kennedy ran off a bridge. Hell, Bush killed 243 Marines and another 69 at the embassy," he says in reference to the administration's policy in Lebanon.

Handicapping the presidential field, Thompson sounds like a police sergeant reading out a rap sheet on each candidate:

Governor Michael Dukakis: "His wife spent twenty-six years as a speed freak. She is more interesting than her husband. She makes Rosalynn Carter look like a charwoman. She should be running."

Senator Albert Gore: "I have no interest in Gore, and I'd be surprised if anybody else does."

Representative Richard Gephardt: "He won't be around by Super Tuesday."

Former governor Bruce Babbitt: "Are you kidding? Really?"

Senator Paul Simon. "I like Simon. I think he's honest in a simple way. But you don't run for president as a simpleton. Look at him. He couldn't win an election for sheriff in most places."

Reverend Jesse Jackson. "My inclination is to vote for Jesse. I like Jesse. He makes politics what it should be." Then, and stressing that he means the words to be complimentary, like a soul brother, he calls Jackson "a wild nigger."

Gorbachev, he says, "could win in Iowa."

No Republicans need apply.

Bush he dismisses as an obsequious geek. "Electing him would be the continuation of Nixon." In one diatribe in the *Examiner*, Thompson wrote that Bush's "face has become swollen and he is said to be plagued by a growth of dead fatty tissue on his back, which is gathering in a lump in the area between his shoulder blades and prevents him from walking normally."

Senator Robert Dole: "Against Bush, I'd make him three-to-one. Electing Dole would be like electing Jim Wright [the Speaker of the House]. It's the Peter Principle at work."

Former governor Pierre S. du Pont: "A dilettante."

Al Haig: "I enjoy Haig. He's crazy as a loon. I like him

like I like Pat Buchanan." In one column, Thompson wrote of "Cruel Crazy Patrick and Big Al, the Wild Boys, roaming around Washington like a pair of Foam Frogs in heat, laying 3,000 eggs every night and cranking up a genuinely mean ticket—Haig & Buchanan, Buchanan & Haig. What does it matter? 'We will kill the ones who eat us, and eat the ones we kill. . . .'"

Representative Jack Kemp: "An airhead stuck with that 'trickle-down' crap."

Reverend Pat Robertson: "He's in it to sell his revival tapes."

Thompson confesses, "My great fear is that it'll go by default to Bush. If Bush wins, we all might as well give up on this country until the year 3000."

Thompson has no apologies for his treatment of Bush, or for his verbal manhandling of Humphrey. Nearly ten years after Humphrey died of cancer, Thompson was excoriating another old New Deal Democrat in a recent column: "Even Hubert Humphrey was shamed, all alone in his unquiet grave down in the depths of the River Styx." Humphrey, he says, "cost us control of the country for ten years." Thompson's only regret is that once he wrote that Humphrey should have been castrated, then later learned that Humphrey had a handicapped grandchild. "I felt bad about that."

It was five below zero outside Thompson's cabin, and the dawn sky was gray as slate. The cabdriver from Mellow Yellow Taxi Co., who had been waiting outside for me, came inside to warm up and pop a Molson for himself.

We were talking about books and, flushed with drink, mortality. Thompson has completed a novel he calls *The*

Night Manager, which he hopes will be published someday. Thompson has had no fiction published, although critics might say that the body of his work should be considered fiction. He particularly admires Joseph Conrad. "He's a gloomy bastard."

I reminded Thompson of his own introduction to *The Great Shark Hunt*, a despondent author's note written on another winter night ten years before when he was contemplating suicide: "I have already lived and finished the life I planned to live (thirteen years longer, in fact) and everything from now on will be A New Life, a different thing . . ."

Thompson replied that he had been unnecessarily morbid at the time; the words were a cryptic reference to his marriage that was failing. He may have been troubled about being forty years old then, but he insisted he doesn't mind being fifty today. There are new politicians to gore, new pomposities to puncture. He is back in command of his career. There is another presidential campaign to cover, and there is no one who can spare the candidates from the wrath of Hunter Thompson.

"I *ENJOY* DRUGS."

INTERVIEW BY WILLIAM MCKEEN
MARCH, 1990

WILLIAM MCKEEN: Your North American articles for the *National Observer* in 1963 seem so much more sedate than your dispatches from South America in 1962 and early 1963. Were there some problems in dealing with the *Observer* when you were closer to the editors?

HUNTER S. THOMPSON: When I came back from South America to the *National Observer*, I came as a man who's been a star—off the plane, all the editors met me and treated me as such. There I was—wild drunk in fatigues and a Panama hat. I said I wouldn't work in Washington. *National Observer* is a Dow Jones company so I continued to write good stories— just without political context.

I drifted West.

MCKEEN: Were there problems in dealing with the *Observer* when you were closer to the editors?

THOMPSON: The *National Observer* became my road gig out of San Francisco. I was too much for them. I would wander in [to the Dow Jones bureau] on off-hours drunk and obviously on drugs asking for my messages. Essentially, they were working for me.

They liked me, but I was the bull in the china shop—the more I wrote about politics, the more they realized who they had on their hands. They knew I wouldn't change and neither would they.

Berkeley, Hells Angels, Kesey, blacks, hippies . . . I had these connections. Rock and roll. I was a crossroads for everything, and they weren't making use of it. I was withdrawn from my news position and began writing book reviews—mainly for money. The final blow was the [Tom] Wolfe review.

I wrote this strongly positive review of Wolfe's *Kandy-Kolored Tangerine-Flake Streamline Baby*. The feature editor killed it because of a grudge. I took the *Observer's* letter and a copy of the review with a brutal letter about it all to Wolfe. I then copied that letter [to Wolfe] and sent it to the *Observer*. I had told Wolfe that the review had been killed for bitchy, personal reasons.

I left to write *Hell's Angels* in 1965.

MCKEEN: What was the nature of the conflict with the *Observer* over the coverage of the Free Speech Movement at Berkeley?

THOMPSON: The Free Speech Movement was virtually non-existent at the time, but I saw it coming. There was a great rumbling—you could feel it everywhere. It was wild, but Dow Jones was just too far away. I wanted to cover the Free Speech Movement, but they didn't want me to go.

MCKEEN: Earlier, you spent some of your time at Time Inc., typing the works of Faulkner, Fitzgerald, and other great writers in an effort to understand their style. What writers have had the greatest influence on you?

THOMPSON: I would type things. I'm very much into rhythm—writing in a musical sense. I like gibberish, if it sings. Every author is different—short sentences, long, no commas, many commas. It helps a lot to understand what you're doing. You're writing, and so were they. It won't fit often—that is, *your* hands don't want to do *their* words—but you're *learning.*

MCKEEN: What writers have had the greatest influence on you?

THOMPSON: Conrad, Hemingway, Twain, Faulkner, Fitzgerald . . . Mailer, Kerouac in the political sense—they were allies. Dos Passos, Henry Miller, Isak Dinesen, Edmund Wilson, Thomas Jefferson.

MCKEEN: Did writing sports have an effect on your writing?

THOMPSON: Huge. Look at the action verbs and the freedom to make up words—as a sports editor, you'll have twenty-two headlines and not that many appropriate words. At the Air Force base [he was sports editor of the *Command Courier* at Eglin Air Force Base in Florida in the late 1950s], I'd have my section: flogs, bashes, edges, nips, whips—after a while you run out of available words. You really get those action verbs flowing.

MCKEEN: I'm curious, because some of the best American writers—Lardner, Hemingway, even Updike—covered sports in one way or another.

THOMPSON: I put it all together once with my farewell to sports writing, but I always come back to it under odd circumstances. Ali, the Kentucky Derby, even the Mint 400 [covered in *Las Vegas*].

MCKEEN: What caused the rift with *Rolling Stone*? Was it something that was building for a while?

THOMPSON: [Jann] Wenner folded Straight Arrow Books shortly before the Saigon piece [about the end of the war in 1975]. I had to write that piece because the war had been such a player in my life for ten years. I needed to see the end of it and be a part of it somehow.

Wenner folded Straight Arrow at a time when they owed me $75,000. I was enraged to find that out. It had been an advance for [*The Great*] *Shark Hunt*. I wrote a seriously vicious letter, finally saying all I was thinking as I was taking off for Saigon.

While in Saigon I found out I'd been fired when Wenner flew into a rage upon receiving the letter. Getting fired didn't mean much to me. I was in Saigon, I was writing—except that I lost health insurance. Here I was in a war zone, and no health insurance.

So essentially I refused to write anything once I found out. I found out when I tried to use my Telex card and it was refused. I called *Rolling Stone* to find out why (perfect phone system right to the end of the war). I talked to [managing editor] Paul Scanlon, who was sitting in for Wenner [who was] off skiing. He told me I was fired, but fixed my Telex card, etc.

The business department had ignored the memo to fire

me because it'd happened too many times before. They didn't want to be bothered with the paperwork, so Wenner's attempt had been derailed.

Anyone who would fire a correspondent on his way to disaster . . . I vowed not to work for them. It was the end of our working relationship except for special circumstances.

About that time, they moved to New York. *Rolling Stone* began to be run by the advertising and business departments and not by the editorial department. It was a financial leap forward for Wenner and *Rolling Stone*, but the editorial department lost any real importance.

You shouldn't work for someone who would fire you en route to a war zone.

I got off the plane [in Saigon] greeted by a huge sign that said, "Anyone caught with more than $100 US currency will go immediately to prison." Imagine how I felt with $30,000 taped to my body. I was a pigeon to carry the *Newsweek* payroll and communication to those in Saigon. I thought we'd all be executed. It was total curfew when we got off the plane so we were herded into this small room with all these men holding machine guns. There I was with three hundred times the maximum money allowance. We got out and I leapt on a motor scooter and told the kid to run like hell. I told Loren [Jenkins, *Newsweek* bureau chief] I wouldn't give him the money until he got me a suite in a hotel. Not an easy task, but he came through.

MCKEEN: Was the break with *Rolling Stone* directly related to the "Great Leap of Faith" article [which Wenner promoted as Thompson's endorsement of Carter for president in 1976]?

THOMPSON: I had already picked up on Carter in '74. It was a special assignment as everything was after Saigon. I was still on the masthead: it was an honor roll of journalists, but the people on it—well, all of them were no longer with *Rolling Stone*. I didn't like that they put on the cover that I *endorsed* Carter. I picked him as a gambler. Endorsing isn't something a journalist should do.

Essentially, the fun factor had gone out of *Rolling Stone*. It was an outlaw magazine in California. In New York it became an establishment magazine, and I have never worked well with people like that.

Today at *Rolling Stone* there are rows and rows of white cubicles, each with its own computer. That's how I began to hate computers. They represented all that was wrong with *Rolling Stone*. It became like an insurance office with people communicating cubicle to cubicle.

But my relationship had ended with the firing. The attempt was enough.

MCKEEN: Your use of drugs is one of the more controversial things about you and your writing. Do you think the use of drugs has been exaggerated by the media?

THOMPSON: Obviously, my drug use is exaggerated or I would be long since dead. I've already outlived the most brutal abuser of our time—Neal Cassady. Me and William Burroughs are the only other ones left. We're the only unrepentant public dope fiends around, and he's seventy years old and claiming to be clean. But he hasn't turned on drugs, like [Timothy] Leary.

MCKEEN: How have drugs affected your perception of the world and/or your writing?

THOMPSON: Drugs usually enhance or strengthen my perceptions and reactions, for good or ill. They've given me the resilience to withstand repeated socks to to my innocence gland. The brutal reality of the politics alone would probably be intolerable without drugs. They've given me the strength to deal with those shocking realities guaranteed to shatter *anyone's* beliefs in the higher idealistic shibboleths of our time and the "American Century." Anyone who covers his beat for twenty years, and that beat is "The Death of the American Dream," needs every goddamned crutch he can find.

Besides, I enjoy drugs. The only trouble they've given me is the people who try to keep me from using them. Res ipsa loquitur. I was, after all, a literary lion last year. [He's referring to an honor from the New York Public Library.]

MCKEEN: Does the media portrayal of you as a "crazy" amuse, inflame, or bore you?

THOMPSON: The media perception of me has always been pretty broad. As broad as the media itself. As a journalist, I somehow managed to break most of the rules and still succeed. It's a hard thing for most of today's journeyman journalists to understand, but only because they can't do it. The smart ones understood immediately. The best people in journalism I've never had any quarrel with. I *am* a journalist and I've never met, as a group, any tribe I'd rather be a part of or that are more fun to be with—in spite of the various punks and sycophants of the press. I'm proud to be a part of the tribe.

It hasn't helped a lot to be a savage comic-book character for the last fifteen years—a drunken screwball who should've been castrated a long time ago. The smart people in the media knew it was a weird exaggeration. The dumb ones took it seriously and warned their children to stay away from me at all costs. The really smart ones understood it was only a censored, kind of toned-down children's-book version of the real thing.

Now we are being herded into the nineties, which looks like it is going to be a true generation of swine, a decade run by cops with no humor, with dead heroes and diminished expectations, a decade that will go down in history as The Gray Area. At the end of the decade no one will be sure of anything except that you must obey the rules. Sex will kill you, politicians lie, rain is poison, and the world is run by whores. These are terrible things to have to know in your life, even if you're rich.

Since that's become the mode, that sort of thinking has taken over the media as it has business and politics: "I'm going to turn you in, son—not only for your own good but because you were the bastard who turned me in last year."

The vilification by Nazi elements within the media has not only given me a fierce joy to continue my work—more and more alone out here, as darkness falls on the barricades— but has also made me profoundly orgasmic, mysteriously rich, and constantly at war with those vengeful retro-fascist elements of the Establishment that have hounded me all my life. It has also made me wise, shrewd, and crazy on a level that can only be known by those who have been there.

MCKEEN: Some libraries classify *Fear and Loathing in Las Vegas* as a travelogue, some classify it as nonfiction, and some classify it as a novel. You refer to it as a failed experiment in Gonzo journalism, yet many critics consider it a masterwork. How would you rate it?

THOMPSON: *Fear and Loathing in Las Vegas* is a masterwork. However, true Gonzo journalism as I conceive it shouldn't be rewritten.

MCKEEN: How would you characterize the book?

THOMPSON: I would classify it, in Truman Capote's words, as a nonfiction novel in that almost all of it was true or did happen. I warped a few things, but it was a pretty accurate picture. It was an incredible feat of balance more than literature. That's why I called it *Fear and Loathing*. It was a pretty pure experience that turned into a very pure piece of writing. It's as good as *The Great Gatsby* and better than *The Sun Also Rises*.

MCKEEN: Your stint as a newspaper columnist [for the *San Francisco Examiner*] was successful, but do you have further ambitions within journalism?

THOMPSON: I've never had any real ambition within journalism, but events and fate and my own sense of fun keep taking me back for money, political reasons, and because I'm a warrior.

MCKEEN: Do you have an ambition to write fiction?

THOMPSON: I've always had and still do have an ambition to write fiction.

MCKEEN: For years your readers have heard about *The Rum Diary*. Are you working on it, or on any other novel?

THOMPSON: *The Rum Diary* is currently under cannibalization and transmogrification into a very strange movie.

I am now working on my final statement—*Polo is My Life*, which is a finely muted saga of sex, treachery, and violence in the 1990s, which also solves the murder of John F. Kennedy.

I haven't found a drug yet that can get you anywhere near as high as sitting at a desk writing, trying to imagine a story no matter how bizarre it is.

"THIS IS NOT A NIGHT TO BE ALONE."

INTERVIEWS BY DAVID STREITFELD
1990–2000

I. DECEMBER, 1990

Hunter's reputation is at a low ebb, and so is he. The master-pieces were long ago, and the general feeling among critics and even some fans is that he is coasting. In the stern culture of the pre-internet era, there is no greater insult. A true artist, it was believed, must continually top himself and not just deliver more of the same.

I was a young reporter for The Washington Post. *I also wrote a freelance column for the paper's book review. I told my girlfriend I'd be back in an hour and went off to see Hunter at the Carlyle Hotel, one of New York's swankiest. My plan was to pick up a few pithy quotes for a column. I did not know then that Hunter never met a deadline.*

For the seven million other people in New York City, it's midafternoon. But for Hunter S. Thompson, it's an unfriendly dawn. Breakfast for six is cooling in his suite's living room, waiting for the star of the show to emerge. Occasional thuds can be heard as he moves around the bedroom, tiny collisions with the environment, which proves at least that he's awake. Not to mention alive.

Few would have bet on it. Back in the early seventies, his physician wrote him a letter saying he'd be dead in a year if he didn't slacken his intake of drugs and alcohol. The doctor then retired, confident in his warning, but recently

Thompson heard from him again: "You have done amazing things since your death sixteen years ago . . ."

Making it through those years would be the principal one. The fifty-one-year-old practitioner of New Journalism who aced the form with *Hell's Angels*, the inventor of Gonzo journalism in the classic *Fear and Loathing in Las Vegas*, the political writer who helped reshape the game with his coverage in *Rolling Stone* of the Nixon-McGovern match, has been reduced in his latest outing, *Songs of the Doomed*, to including snippets of unpublished novels and documents pertaining to a drug bust at his Colorado home.

From a literary point of view, in fact, it's been a slide ever since his doctor told him he was done for. Maybe the doc was speaking metaphorically. Even Thompson's latest gig, writing a column for the *San Francisco Examiner*, has come to an end in a welter of accusations about expenses.

"I think I'd better get back to writing for money pretty quick, or I might die," he says in a letter to his agent that is lying on one of the tables in the suite. "I feel like a junkie who got trapped by accident in the Baghdad airport on the day of the Kuwait invasion—with no sleep, no cash, and just enough drugs to make it through the long flight to Rome . . . And then . . .

"What do you mean . . . the flight's cancelled?!"

Two publicists are lingering, waiting only for Thompson to appear before they can disappear. They both have places to go on this Friday before Christmas, and in addition both are ill. In the meantime, they answer the phone. A waiter has brought up more eggs, the first batch having been deemed over-poached. The rejects lie scattered around the

room, plump little white pods that could star in a remake of
Invasion of the Body Snatchers.

The phone rings for the tenth time. It's Jane Wenner,
wife of Jann, the owner of *Rolling Stone.* Jann Wenner himself has called. Despite their regular public denunciations of
each other, Jann and Thompson go back too far, and their
reputations are too wrapped up in each other, for them to be
anything but friends.

Thompson is talking on the phone in the bedroom to
someone else. Out in the world, people are leaving work early,
finishing their Christmas shopping, hanging the stockings
by the chimney with care. In Suite 822 of the Carlyle, which
goes for $600 a night, the new eggs are cold. One of the pub-
licists sets about reheating them in the kitchen.

Eventually, the door to the bedroom opens. It's not a
grand entrance, but at this stage no one is picky. "This is just
so crazy," Thompson mutters by way of introduction. "I'll
never travel again without a huge staff. You should see how I
was yesterday, with no one."

He walks around the room, bottle of Chivas Regal in
hand. With its trays of food, the room resembles an obstacle
course. Thompson moves jerkily, as if his body weren't quite
used to locomotion. "Anyone want any of this food?" he says
to no one in particular. "There's a lot here." His eggs are cold
again.

The phone rings. It's for him.

"I was hopeless yesterday," he says into the mouthpiece.
"I kept bumping into things, cracked my knee on the TV set,
all kinds of terrible things . . . Did you go to that George
Plimpton thing last night? I was going to go and I just crashed."

He sneezes. And again. "All I fucking need now." And
again. "I'm allergic to the telephone . . . Call me later."

Thompson has propped open the door to the hallway,
and now opens a window. "Gotta create a wind tunnel effect,"
he says vaguely. Freezing air begins to move through the
room. One of the publicists manages to slip away. Before the
other can leave, she needs Thompson to sign a huge poster
advertising *Songs of the Doomed* for the Hard Rock Café. This
is easier said than done. For one thing, he can't find a flat
writing surface big enough to lay the poster on.

A low scream issues from his belly, and he nimbly flips
one of the Villeroy & Boch breakfast plates off the coffee
table and onto one of the room service carts, where it shat-
ters. At least some space has been cleared. Unfortunately,
the publicist has one more thing for him to sign, and the
reaction is the same. This time he throws his pen. It hits several finely spun miniature carafes of tomato juice, breaking
the necks off.

Writing, it seems, does not come easily to Thompson
these days. The cover of *Songs of the Doomed* shows him
shooting a typewriter. Quite a change from his heyday, when
his pistol was a pen, or as he immodestly put it in 1975, "I am
one of the best writers currently using the English language
as both a musical instrument and a political weapon."

The phone rings again. It is *The New York Times*, calling
to see if he will write an op-ed piece. He has already lined up
a regular column with *Esquire*. He will soon be going to the
Soviet Union, a trip he says he will write up for *Rolling Stone*.
There is a book in preparation on his drug trial. And he's eager
to complete a novel, *Polo Is My Life*.

From the letter to his agent: "I feel in the mood to write a long weird story—a tale so strange & terrible that it will change the brain of the normal reader forever . . . Which is not a crime—but almost, in some precincts—and in Arizona they hang you for it.

"So what?

"A lot of bad weird things happen in Arizona. Power moves very nakedly in that corner of the desert, and only the rich survive to tell their side of the story . . . Every time I fly into Phoenix, for instance, I expect to be killed. Not immediately. Not at the airport. But almost any time after that . . . Hell, you never know in Arizona. Some people get killed and some don't . . . But even if you get out alive, you always know somebody wanted to kill you; they just didn't get around to it, this time."

This is a nice piece of Gonzo writing. The writer agrees, offers to have a bellman go out and make copies. The last publicist is gone, despite Thompson's pleas to remain. The phone is ringing. It's his girlfriend, who is trapped in Colorado by a snowstorm and is finding herself unable to join him. He is distraught about the prospect of not seeing her, or maybe just at the notion of being alone.

When Thompson's not moving, he still looks solid enough to kick the daylights out of an office candy machine, which is how he got fired from the *Middletown Daily Record* about 1960 or so. The hair is sparse—most of it, according to one account, fell out more than twenty-five years ago due to "repeated dosages of speed and cortisone and fear"—but the eyes can still make contact. When he's not shouting, he's capable of calming down into something resembling amiability.

At a very early point during his youth in Kentucky, he says, "I could see myself getting into patterns where I wouldn't have to worry about a Social Security card." When he was nine, his grandmother set up an account for him at Louisville Trust. Shortly thereafter, young Hunter withdrew all the money. "Last time I ever had a savings account," he says. "I guess I do have some life insurance I got a long time ago. I guess I couldn't get it if they knew who I was."

He has no great philosophic ruminations about why he turned out this way. Between 1962 and 1975, he writes in *Songs of the Doomed,* "I managed—by using almost any kind of valid or invalid journalistic credentials I could get my hands on—to get myself personally involved in just about everything that interested me: from Berkeley to Chicago, Las Vegas to the White House, shark-fishing, street-fighting, dope-smuggling, Hell's Angels, Super Bowls, local politics, and a few things I'd prefer not to mention until various statutes of limitations expire."

Risking his life in the process, he says now, "wasn't a conscious decision, just more fun . . . I never meant to become famous for high-wire dancing, but I'm afraid I've become addicted to my own adrenaline."

It also pays the bills. The new book, which consists of uncollected pieces over the last thirty years plus a running commentary linking them together, is doing moderately well; his previous collection of articles, *Generation of Swine,* in 1988, was a bona fide bestseller. And there's always money to be made on the college circuit, where he is celebrated by youths who weren't born when Thompson made his name covering events in such deranged fashion you never knew what was the truth, and didn't care either. *Fear and Loathing in Las Vegas*, his most sustained performance, begins like this:

"We were somewhere around Barstow on the edge of the desert when the drugs began to take hold. I remember saying something like 'I feel a bit lightheaded; maybe you should drive . . .' And suddenly there was a terrible roar all around us and the sky was full of what looked like huge bats, all swooping and screeching and diving around the car, which was going about a hundred miles an hour with the top down to Las Vegas. And a voice was screaming: 'Holy Jesus! What are these goddamn animals?'"

Even now, asked how much reality entered into his crazed exploits while simultaneously covering a motorcycle race in the desert and a drug conference of district attorneys, he will merely say, "It's dangerous to answer that one." Perhaps he means dangerous to his reputation; perhaps *Fear and Loathing* is a novel and that likewise the rather mild events of this afternoon, with Thompson letting out a primal scream every time the phone rings and busting the crockery whenever the opportunity presents itself, are only the writer trying to keep his myth intact.

The phone rings. It's the guy from *The New York Times* again. A *Times* reporter who did a recent feature on Thompson is also trying to get in touch, as is a writer doing a profile of the *Rolling Stone* essayist P. J. O'Rourke. Call back, everyone is told.

Besides the college crowd, which knows a party animal when it sees one, Thompson is a defiant hero to journalists who have been told by their editors to keep a close watch on expense accounts in these recessionary times. His definition of restraint: "I don't have wild parties or charge tuxedos to the hotel, but I do bitch when I can't get a laundry bag full of cash to leave the country immediately. I don't work long for people who don't pay the expenses, let's put it that way."

Speaking of which, it's time for more room service. His supply of Chivas is vanishing rapidly, and you never can tell when you'll run out of beer. "A small pitcher of orange juice, six Heinekens, a bottle of Chivas Regal . . . a bucket of ice. What sort of desserts you got down there? Tortes? Fruit tarts? And two dozen long-stemmed roses."

He pauses again, during which time the room service operator, clearly realizing he has a live one on the line, asks if there's anything else they can do for their guest, anything at all. "This is fun, isn't it?" Thompson asks. But the only other thing he can come up with is a rather weak request for "an afternoon paper," of which New York does not exactly boast an abundance.

By now it's night. There remains a special topic Thompson wants to talk about—his arrest in February for allegedly fondling a journalist, subsequent to which his Woody Creek, Colorado, home was raided and a bit of cocaine, some LSD, and a couple of sticks of dynamite were discovered. He beat the sexual assault and drug raps—the prosecutor dropped the charges right as the trial was beginning—but is still incensed at the whole matter.

"I thought if I ever had to go to the Supreme Court, it would be because of the First Amendment." That's the one about Thompson's freedom to call someone "a lying Nazi bastard" in print. These days, however, it's the Fourth

Amendment he's concerned about, which is the one concerning unreasonable search and seizure. "If they can come and get me in Woody Creek," he says, "they can get the bastard in the next creek over."

He's thinking about suing the government, and has set up a Fourth Amendment Foundation. "The Constitution," he declares, "is not just a document in Philadelphia somewhere, but it should have prevented them from coming in."

There's a knock on the door. Thompson, who has forgotten all about ordering room service, gives a little yelp. Clearly, this is not someone you should sneak up on and tap on the shoulder. The waiter brings in the cart. There is no room; one of the breakfast carts will have to go. The waiter eyes the broken plate. "Sorry," says Thompson guilelessly. "Something happened."

The phone rings. There's another knock on the door. It's the guy with the roses. Truly, an impressive bunch of flowers. Of course, for $270.63—the total on the attached bill—they had better be. Like the waiter, the man who brought the flowers leaves without a tip.

"I don't even have time to abuse myself, these days," Thompson says. He means with drugs. "I'm an addictive personality, but I'm also addicted to functioning. I consider myself essentially a road man for the boys upstairs, the Lords of Karma."

From these random statements, the conversation slides into talk about his mother, Virginia Ray Thompson. "She was always worried about me. 'Why don't you get a job? Why are you being arrested all the time?' It took her a while to realize I was a writer. She still tongue-waxes me . . . It terrifies me that my mother's eighty-four. You want to be eighty-four?"

Considering the alternative, yes. Hunter Thompson,

however, has made his living by dancing on the edge. Recently, it's true, the abyss seems to be winning. There's a line in *Songs of the Doomed* about a man whose "brain was so rotted with drink and dissolute living that whenever he put it to work it behaved like an old engine that had gone haywire from being dipped in lard." That, his detractors say, is a self-portrait.

But perhaps Thompson, having made it this far, might just surprise everyone and pull off his big book. He describes *Polo Is My Life* as "just a good, old-fashioned love story, like *Psycho* or *Blue Velvet*." He wants $9 million for it. He says he's got a dinner lined up with Sonny Mehta, the president of Alfred A. Knopf and recently a very successful publisher with some money to spare. Perhaps, perhaps.

First, though, there's some serious partying to be done. When Thompson is last seen, he is talking on the phone. A chill wind blows through the room. There are empty beer bottles everywhere, and little pieces of glass on the floor. "Why don't you come over?" he is saying. "This is not a night to be alone."

I got back to my girlfriend about six hours late. Gentleman that he was, Hunter insisted I take her all those roses, wrapped up in a Carlyle towel. I crept through the lobby, sure I'd be arrested for stealing hotel property, but no one batted an eye.

II. SUMMER, 1994

Another expensive hotel suite, this time at the Ritz-Carlton in Washington, DC. Thompson's new book was Better Than Sex:

Confessions of a Political Junkie, *a hodgepodge of memos, musings, faxes to the Clinton campaign and his friend Ed Turner, plus clippings, a timeline, quotations set off in bold type and other forms of marginalia, all stitched together with a running commentary on the recent presidential election.*

Despite his protests that he was dragged unwillingly into covering the campaign, it energized him. Two decades earlier, Fear and Loathing on the Campaign Trail *showed what happened when the bad guys won.* Better Than Sex *is about the triumph of the good guys, but this does not turn out much happier. The Clintons were the first of Thompson's generation to achieve power, and their enemies were his enemies. But the writer was ambivalent about Bill and Hillary from the start, and often outright negative. Clinton versus George Bush in 1992, Thompson wrote, was a rerun of 1976: "Another self-righteous, New Age, boll-weevil Southern Democrat against another greedy, dimwit, corrupt, caretaker Republican."*

One of Thompson's all-time best lines came during the campaign. Clinton admitted he had smoked marijuana but maintained he had not inhaled. Asked about this by The New York Times, *Thompson replied, "Only a fool would say a thing like that. It's just a disgrace to an entire generation."*

Some of the things he wrote in Better Than Sex *were not only true then but seem like they always will be, like this: "There is no such thing as paranoia in a presidential campaign. Anything you fear or suspect will almost always turn out to be true, and the fix is always in, somewhere, and the enemy of your enemy is not always your friend. And that, for the true campaign junkie, is precisely what makes it fun."*

When this interview took place, the Whitewater controversy—a complicated land deal in backwoods Arkansas that, stoked by the right wing, bedeviled the Clintons forever—had just claimed a major victim. Deputy Treasury Secretary Roger Altman resigned after it came out that he had been less than completely truthful in Congressional testimony about the matter. Thompson had a few things to say about this.

He began by brandishing a toy roach, waving it at me and a few groupies who were also present. Then he used a marker to draw a black box on the suite's white carpet. He carefully positioned his bug inside the box.

THOMPSON: The trick here is to pretend the roach is a scorpion. Now gentlemen, you have to imagine you're in the Caribbean. And you have to imagine you just put your coat on, and out through the sleeve came a huge scorpion. I tell you, "Don't worry about scorpions. Here's what we do with them here: you grab a stick, and in the sand draw a box around the scorpion."

The scorpion will rush everywhere, trying to get out, trying to make it over the wall. And scorpions can't jump. *[Laughs wildly.]* That popped out of nowhere. They have hideous tails. The poison is not totally fatal, but it will hurt you. Anyway, it gets so frustrated at rushing around that it finally goes nuts, and stings itself to death.

STREITFELD: Really?

THOMPSON: That's true. Well, this is what they tell you in the Caribbean. You just have to draw, you know, the classic line in the sand.

STREITFELD: Hunter, is this a metaphor?

THOMPSON: Look at it this way: scorpions are at best a half-inch tall. More like a quarter-inch. And the tail's at best a half-inch long. So the crevice looks much bigger to a scorpion than it does to us. To the scorpion, it looks deep. No one has ever seen a scorpion jump. People actually amuse themselves by catching a scorpion and playing with it like this on Aruba.

STREITFELD: Have you?

THOMPSON: I've never trapped a scorpion and witnessed it sting itself to death. But then, neither have I . . . [*Pause*] . . . I have not . . . [*Pause*] . . . stabbed myself through the palm to produce a stigmata to convince someone I love them. Okay, I know that's weak.

STREITFELD: You believe this, right?

THOMPSON: I tend to believe it. There's a lot of folklore I'm not sure I believe, like George Washington actually throwing a dollar across the Potomac. Spiro Agnew, maybe. He probably threw some cash in a brown paper bag. But I believe this. It's a metaphor for life, and it's a metaphor for the Clinton White House.

[He makes a half-hearted effort to rub the ink off the carpet, fails, goes back to the couch.]

That was a lot of work to get my message across. We understand that [Clinton aide] George Stephanopoulos is a scorpion. And that Roger Altman was stung to death. The whole Clinton administration is like a scorpion in a box. Ronald Reagan was not. He was a scorpion who could jump. Nothing about the town bothered him at all. Except when Frank Sinatra came to town.

STREITFELD: Frank Sinatra?

THOMPSON: And then there was Nixon—I think he liked it here. He hated to leave, I know that now. I was the last person in the line the day he left in 1974, at the end of the red carpet. I was given a choice between being inside and hearing the speech about how my mother was a saint, and being outside, on the red carpet, saying goodbye. I choose to go outside. It was a rainy, muggy day, and they had the red carpet going all the way to to the helicopter. I was the last person in the line.

Nixon was so doped up, sort of like O. J. Simpson during the slow speed chase. He was almost comatose. I remember feeling sorry for him. It was a moment of terrible weakness. Or maybe I was there just to make sure he left. I nodded at him as he went by. We got Nixon on a technicality. At the time it was a hugely important thing, but now I think Iran-Contra was worse.*

---

*To put the kindest interpretation on this, Hunter's memory seems faulty. According to Craig Vetter, who was interviewing the writer that summer for a piece in *Playboy*, he and Hunter saw Nixon leave the White House for the last time the same way most of America did, on TV. They were in a bar in the Watergate Hotel.

[The phone rings.]

Hey, c'mon now, someone's going to have to deal with that!

[No one moves. It continues to ring].

What is it, some kind of warning for the fucking CIA creep out there?

[He finally answers. It is Clinton adviser James Carville, checking in.]

James! We were just talking about you. We were talking about scorpions in the sand and how they sting themselves to death in frustration. Are you back in town? Having any fun?

[They agree to talk later and Thompson hangs up.]

STREITFELD: So, your point is that the Clinton administration screwed up by not being aggressive enough?

THOMPSON: Yeah. "Why" is harder than "how." Roger Altman had an opportunity to kick the GOP out of the box. The economy's recovering, allegedly. There are many more jobs. The deficit is down for the first time since Reagan was president. "What are you doing bothering me?" Altman should have said. "You bother me with this gossip? We came to Washington for a different, better purpose." Doesn't that seem simple? The White House had an argument. It may be

bogus in the end. But you know the old adage, "Let's make
the bastards deny it."

[He recounted an anecdote from Better Than Sex about an
early campaign of Lyndon Johnson's against a wealthy pig
farmer: "The year was 1948, as I recall, and Lyndon was
running about ten points behind, with only nine days to
go . . . He called his equally depressed campaign manager
and instructed him to call a press conference at 2:00 or 2:30
(just after lunch on a slow news day) and accused his high-
riding opponent (the pig farmer) of having routine carnal
knowledge of his barnyard sows.

'We can't say that, Lyndon,' the campaign manager said.
'It's not true.'

'Of course it's not,' Johnson said, 'but let's make the bastard deny it.']

It's a basic rule of politics. The Republicans would have
to say, "What do you mean, it's gossip?" Let them deny they
created the savings and loan problem. "You have the nerve to
subpoena me up here? What's wrong with you?" That's what
Altman should have said.

Politics has changed. Altman went into one of these—
[literally crouches in mock fear]—"Don't hit me!" Oh, well. I
was going to send this advice to Stephanopoulos but someone told me it was too little too late.

STREITFELD: You have mixed feelings about President
Clinton, don't you?

THOMPSON: I didn't like Clinton. I thought he was necessary to beat President Bush, but [billionaire independent candidate] Ross Perot was the one who struck me as a creature of possibility. He just needed a little humor, a little energy. And I liked the idea that there would be three stages of chaos if nobody got enough electoral votes. So I tried to be an elector for all three parties.

STREITFELD: A lot of people were hot on Perot for a while.

THOMPSON: The bottom line here may be that we are a nation of swine. When I said years ago how low you had to stoop to be president I was just ahead of my time.

STREITFELD: What was the last president you were happy to live under?

THOMPSON: Nixon. But that was for the fun of it.

STREITFELD: Maybe *you* should run.

THOMPSON: I may be the cleanest person in the country. Every crime you've ever thought of, I've already admitted I did it.

STREITFELD: Let's talk about literature for a moment.

THOMPSON: I am now part of the Twayne series on modern American writers.

STREITFELD: They did a scholarly volume on you? I can't believe they're letting Gonzo into the establishment!

THOMPSON: What do you mean? It's about the work. My mother's a librarian in Louisville. Being in the Twayne series is the only thing I've done that's impressed her.

STREITFELD: There are a bunch of biographies of you coming out.

THOMPSON: Three of them. Seemed crazy to me. They must have been betting on my death. Some sort of lottery, I guess.

STREITFELD: You're not dead yet.

THOMPSON: I ran into Keith Richards, and I got his secret about changing my blood to keep me young.

STREITFELD: Let's go back to politics.

THOMPSON: The Clinton transition really turned me off. I kept thinking, "He'll be better than this. He'll justify my endorsement." I kept waiting. Goddamn, it's been a long wait.

STREITFELD: It might be a long time still.

THOMPSON: The Rolling Stones have been on the road for thirty years. I'm not there yet, but I've been covering politics since 1968. I didn't really think I was going back to it. It's not because I was drawn back in by a surge of nostalgic loyalty. Or the old cause. Or because I saw the colors raised again.

And Clinton didn't like me. I didn't like Clinton before I met him, I didn't like him after I met him, but I thought he could beat George Bush.

I don't think Clinton likes anything I stand for.

STREITFELD: But he likes to have a good time, like you.

THOMPSON: In a different way than I do. He's not much fun. I think the next election is thrown. That's the way it looks now. Bob Dole is frontrunner. He's a party man but an impeccable politician. He's a warrior. You have to admire Dole. Also, he looks ten years younger than Teddy Kennedy.

STREITFELD: Dole seems kind of mean.

THOMPSON: Whoever told you politics was a bunch of friendly people?

STREITFELD: What exactly do you have against Clinton?

THOMPSON: He has no roots, no groundings, no convictions. Even his taste is bad taste. Clinton has the midnight taste of a man who would go on a double date with the Reverend Jimmy Swaggart.* He has the convictions of a kid who wanted to be president. He got on the train of grants and Fulbrights, visited the White House, worked for it. He didn't

*Prominent televangelist who was defrocked by the Assemblies of God after a scandal with a prostitute.

work at anything else. The most money he ever made before he became president was $35,000 a year.

STREITFELD: How early did you suspect things were going downhill?

THOMPSON: The transition was a painful education. You know when Hamilton Jordan said during the Carter campaign, "If we go through all of this and someone like Cyrus Vance ends up as Secretary of State, it won't have been worth the effort." Sure as shit, Cyrus Vance ended up as Secretary of State. With Clinton, Warren Christopher ended up as Secretary of State. The Democratic party is clearly bankrupt, like the Whigs. The Whigs had Henry Clay, Daniel Webster, and John Calhoun. That was the leadership, and they still destroyed themselves. The Democrats haven't had anyone like that. Not any statesmen, even bogus ones.

STREITFELD: Hillary is upset with you, I hear, because of something that happened during the McGovern campaign.

THOMPSON: There was an incident, long ago. I didn't tear the place up. I may not have been an ideal guest. I think I was driving across the lawn. But you have to remember this was a time of great despair for the McGovern staffers, and for blowing off steam. Not that that would excuse driving across lawns. We may have set fire to a Christmas tree. Something like that. I don't recall anything, and it wasn't that bad. We didn't smash stuff up or trash it like a hotel room. I was shocked she would hold a grudge that long.

I was more important to the McGovern campaign than the Clintons were. If I wanted to fire up a Christmas tree, yeah, why not? I didn't do it alone. Eleanor [McGovern's wife] probably helped me.

STREITFELD: How's your health?

THOMPSON: I never expected to be here this long. I planned from early on to die at the age of twenty-seven, actually planned it. Most of the people who knew me were betting on twenty-two. So everything after that's been kind of a shock. I drew my own line in the sand, like a scorpion, on the jacket copy of *Better Than Sex.*

STREITFELD: The jacket says, "He will be gone by the year 2000."

THOMPSON: I didn't want to do the book. They said it will be easy, but there's no such thing as a free lunch, as they say. I had all these faxes. It never occurred to me I was going to have to write an ending. This is my last book on politics.

STREITFELD: Why?

THOMPSON: Well, you have to learn something. Even scorpions learn—well, maybe not. I guess scorpions don't learn. But this book was not fun. Writing, if you care about the writing, is hard. That's why I've done so well with Nixon. Because the majesty of his evil challenged my talent. I recognized the real thing when I saw it.

Nixon was a cut above almost anyone in politics. I think Bob Dole is not as inherently evil as Nixon was. Dole is mean, but he's like a soldier. I respect his professionalism, and I have to be a professional myself after all this time. I don't clip coupons, I don't sell drugs. I don't have any other income except as a writer.

This didn't even seem like a book at first. It seemed like *The Diary of Anne Frank*—something that somebody would find and steal and publish. I thought of doing it all holographic, to make it more convincing.

STREITFELD: What? Oh, you mean handwritten. Is it hard to remain an outlaw in this culture?

THOMPSON: I seem to be doing pretty well. But yeah, it is hard. I like to think I've learned.

STREITFELD: What have you learned?

THOMPSON: Oh, goddamn you. I haven't learned to stay away from politics. I'm an addictive personality. That's what this is all about, really.

STREITFELD: Is it hard to be Hunter Thompson?

THOMPSON: It is, but there's no point in bitching about it. Some would say, "What's so hard about it? You haven't had a job in twenty years. You get paid to do whatever you want to do."

STREITFELD: I talked to [*Rolling Stone* editor] Bob Love. He told me that you were in such good shape these days, you were "striking a blow for clearheadedness." Or maybe you just renegotiated your pact with the Devil. And Ed Turner [a CNN vice-president who was a Hunter pen pal] said, "There is a saint, a god, a patron somewhere who lets a few sneak through the hurdles that kill you and me."

THOMPSON: It seems to me like only two or three long years since I was twenty-two. Only the passing of Nixon made me feel old. I don't have any real respect for living a long time. I feel sorry for my mother. She's eighty-nine. She's sharp, but she's old, and having a hard time. Her friends are dying. There's no point in living that long, particularly in a world where one year could be the equivalent of living ten years in the 1940s or '50s. It used to take days for people around the country to learn who was nominated for president. Everything happens fast now.

STREITFELD: But meanwhile there is work to be done.

THOMPSON: I have been discreetly accepting applications for the post of editorial assistant for my next book. It's a hard dollar. I don't dare advertise it. *[Brandishes piece of paper.]* This came from a fifteen-year-old girl. My readership seems to have jumped two or three generations. I don't quite grasp it, but it is true. So this letter was written by a fifteen-year-old girl who had been in bad company, living with adoptive parents. She's now sixteen. A girl who was into robbing morgues with gangs of her friends. She's over the worship-of-the-dead thing. She is a good poet. I don't think I can possibly think about having her come work for me. She's a very precocious teenager. I wrote some good stuff when I was sixteen, but nothing like this. This is an old soul, as they say.

STREITFELD: I can see why she likes you.

THOMPSON: Because I'm almost dead? It helps to be a little bit weird. You gotta have something. Although it's getting harder to be weird. Think of all this PC shit. You know, "weird" is one of those words I always had a hard time spelling. "Weird" and "sheriff." I finally got to remember "weird" by remembering it's "we" and "ird." Weird.

STREITFELD: So what we have here is a kinder and gentler Hunter Thompson.

THOMPSON: Oh, God. Just look what happened to the last guy who said that. Anyway, you wouldn't say that if you had any idea of what I've been doing. I listen on the internet. They don't know I'm there. Billy Idol put his address on the internet and got twenty million responses. If I'm there in any form it'll be as a fifteen-year-old girl.

For no particular reason, Hunter starts throwing the fruit from the fruit basket into the garbage can. He misses, then misses again. Soon there is an orange, apples, a banana on the floor. He throws his package of cigarettes.

THOMPSON: How'd you like to play for money? A hundred dollars an apple.

The groupies laugh and Hunter gets mad.

THOMPSON: It just won't go in. There's a lid on the basket. Showing off is bad karma. Look, I made a total ass of myself. If you're not doing it for the money, you get sloppy.

He keeps trying. Soon, there are fruit smears on the wall.

THOMPSON: This is the last shot. If I don't make it now, we've failed. We're zero.

The apple goes in. Victory at last.

III. FEBRUARY 1999

The late Clinton years showed a resurgent Hunter. He stopped trying to produce new collections but basked in the reverence paid to Hell's Angels *and* Fear and Loathing in Las Vegas, *now old enough to be classics. The Proud Highway, a thick volume of letters, showcased his long apprenticeship in the early 1960s, when he was full of energy and ambition, if not much success. It sold well and got impressive reviews. Johnny Depp's film adaptation of* Las Vegas *received mixed notices but was still enshrinement by Hollywood, the closest thing to immortality that American culture has to offer.*

Hunter was also somewhat vindicated by Bill Clinton, who

disappointed much of the country just the way the writer antici-
pated. The president's impeachment inspired some of the writer's
finest invective. I talked to Hunter by phone and filed an update.

Hunter Thompson, who tends to see things in apocalyptic terms, had dire forebodings about the trial of President
Clinton. "If he walks, the bloodbath will begin immediately
and continue for twenty-five moons," the Gonzo journalist
wrote me a month ago. "James Carville will march on a road
of bones and geeks like Hyde, Starr, and Helms will be hung
by piano wire from the top of the Washington Monument. It
will be a pogrom."

That sounded like just the sort of wildness that
Thompson, who first established a reputation as an offbeat
political commentator during Nixon's long decline, would
relish being a part of. But while he spent some time in late
December debating whether or not to reserve a suite at the
Dupont Circle hotel he still calls the Ritz-Carlton, he never
quite managed to do it.

"Not for me, bubba," he wrote. "I am off to Cuba in a few
days, flying on a private jet out of Little Rock. Don't ask why.
We are, after all, professionals."

He was torn, he told me from his Colorado farm. "I'd
like to come. I know I should come." Clinton's trial, he noted,
was a major historical event, "like the battle of Gettysburg.
And it's exciting. When Livingston resigned"—Republican
Rep. Bob Livingston was in line to become House speaker
until it was revealed he had an extramarital affair—"you
could see the shock among news people in Washington. They

looked like they'd been hit on the back with a two-by-four."

But ultimately, the whole show felt a bit like a rerun. "Only a person suffering from a severe political jones and getting paid very well would be there. It would be like going to hell for Christmas."

For a long time after the appearance of his signature work—*Fear and Loathing in Las Vegas* and the 1972 political coverage—Thompson seemed more of a performance artist than a writer. Getting him to produce anything was a famous editorial ordeal. The work of the eighties echoed his best stuff, it didn't top it. Critics said he was burned out, a parody.

That was then. Now he's practically an elder statesman of literature. The first volume of his collected letters was hailed as some of his sharpest writing, which tended to underestimate the shock value of the whole project: when was the last time a volume of letters by a living writer was even published by a major house, let alone got on the bestseller lists?

The movie adaptation of *Fear and Loathing*, starring Johnny Depp, was disliked enough to get on some critics' worst-of-the-year lists, but at least it wasn't the sentimental cookie-cutter claptrap that Hollywood usually produces. Meanwhile, that book appeared in a Modern Library classics edition—no longer quite the honor it once was, but still something. Thompson recently did an introduction to *Gonzo the Art*, a collection by his longtime illustrator Ralph Steadman, calling him "the Albert Gore of late twentieth-century art."

Finally, last fall saw the appearance of *The Rum Diary: The Long Lost Novel*. The subtitle is a misnomer. The book was never lost, just unsalable. He began it in 1959, when he was twenty-two and had been working for, of all things, a bowling magazine in Puerto Rico. Like every literary young man then, Thompson wanted to write the Great American Novel. "In a twisted way," he promised a friend, *The Rum Diary* "will do for San Juan what *The Sun Also Rises* did for Paris."

The novel is narrated by Paul, who goes to the island to work on a failing newspaper. There's not much plot, but a lot of wild behavior, plus some existential angst ("We were all actors, kidding ourselves along a senseless odyssey.") It's also nicely compact, barely two hundred pages.

Originally, it was longer, which might have been a reason why it didn't sell. "I got all kinds of letters from publishers saying it showed promise, but it was very sloppy and repetitive. I was making my case over and over." Thompson didn't suffer such criticism well. To an agent who declined to represent him, he wrote, "I think we are coming to a day when agents of your sort will serve no useful function except as punching bags."

Cutting the book for publication was a worthwhile learning experience. "Sometimes the best parts are the ones you leave out. Like in this documentary I was watching about black and white films, where they said the best lights in a scene are the ones you don't turn on."

The behavior of the characters in *Rum Diary* is so crazed it resembles, well, Thompson's own exploits. But he maintains it's not a roman a clef. "I'm not in there. Well, okay, I'm in there a lot. That's fair." The trouble was, he put aspects of his real-life personality into both the narrator and another character, with the result that they both talk in the same voice.

So it's not a masterpiece, but it's still something more than a curiosity—a worthwhile addition to the Thompson shelf. It sold better than 99 percent of all the other first novels published last year, but didn't quite crack the bestseller list. "I guess putting that 'long lost novel' on the cover screwed up the sales, what do you think?"

In a recent sketch, "Reflections on Fuel, Madness and Music," he writes that the Robert Mitchum picture *Thunder Road* was "one of those movies that got a grip on me when I was too young to resist. It convinced me that the only way to drive was at top speed with a car full of whiskey, and I have been driving that way ever since, for good or ill."

I used to interview Thompson every once in a while because I knew he'd soon be dead, and that way I'd be ready for the obituary. Now I figure he'll probably outlive me. His first grandchild was born last year.

"I've already given him drugs," he said proudly. Told that people might take this comment at face value, he retreated. "Sure, think I'm going to give four new generations a handle to flog me with?"

In between watching the impeachment and trial ("I have several bets that we'll soon see Clinton and Monica together, window-shopping in Paris"), he's been working on a CD of certain favorite songs. "This is a good album, an energy package. I could sell this at the health foods store." Does he sing on it? "Of course not." The selections are by Lou Reed, Bob Dylan, Rod Stewart and others.

It's called, somewhat obscurely, *Where Were You When the Fun Stopped*. Said Thompson, "I never have enough fun. That's when you get old—you think you have enough fun.

On an hour-to-hour, day-to-day basis, I'm always looking for fun." For the first time ever, though, he has a mild sense of restraint. "I have to. You try being a whirling dervish for fifty years."

The trial, he correctly anticipated, was not going to be fun. No wonder he didn't come. But for the record, here's how he sees the future: "Two chickens in every pot, new Oldsmobiles everywhere, one cop for every citizen, rich generals dropping bombs on a whim, and Bill Clinton back in the White House by 2004."

IV. OCTOBER 2000.

I went to see Hunter at Owl Farm in Woody Creek just as Americans were poised to decide between Al Gore and George Bush. It seemed to many that the choice was over personalities, not policies, and hardly worth bothering about. That was a sharp contrast to the period covered in the second volume of Hunter's letters, Fear and Loathing in America, *which had just been published. The letters began in January 1968 and ended in November 1976, nine years of turmoil that spanned four presidents.*

Those were the years when Hunter did his best work, developed the notion of Gonzo journalism, created an image and was trapped by it. "I got what they call an 'adult dose' of American political reality in an era when the nation seemed to be going up in flames every day of every week," he wrote in an author's note to the collection, adding: "In a four-year span I was teargassed or beaten or chased like a rat by police about two hundred times in at least twenty states, from Key Biscayne to the Olympic

Peninsula, from Gainesville & Miami to Montreal & Austin &
the gates of Beverly Hills. I had such a steady diet of riot-control
gas that I became a junkie, & I still get nostalgic for it on slow
nights."

His subject, then and forever, was the death of the American
Dream. He had a book contract but the topic was so embedded
in the news of the day—the war, the assassinations, Nixon, and
the fragmenting culture—that he could not see it clearly. "Many
words & no focus; that's my epitaph for the past three years," he
complained to his editor in 1970. A few months later, he was
writing "The Kentucky Derby Is Decadent and Depraved," his
first hit in the Gonzo style. He described the article to his agent
as "a classic of the narrative art" and suggested it could be a great
film that melded Dr. Strangelove *and* Gone With the Wind—
two very different American epics. He had found the way in.

During my visit Hunter, sixty-three, was having more trou-
ble than ever moving around, but was still immensely strong. His
consumption of Chivas Regal remained prodigious. I was there
for a few nights, only catching his attention intermittently as
hangers-on came and went, which explains the somewhat frag-
mentary nature to what follows.

He stayed in his command post in the kitchen, wearing a
white bathrobe and red towel. Glasses were perched on the end
of his nose. Several TVs played soundlessly. The weather was
cool but the air conditioning roared. Owl Farm really seemed a
bunker—there was hardly any natural light. Above a doorway
was a sign: "Rage rage against the coming of the light." A plate
of deviled eggs and grapes were on the counter for nibbling, but
I never saw Hunter touch them.

Trying to prove he could still write something beyond a

screed, he was actually reporting a story. A few months earlier, a young man named Jonathan Burton caused a disturbance on a Southwest Airlines flight from Las Vegas to Salt Lake City. The nineteen-year-old Burton, who had no history of mental illness or threatening behavior, tried to enter the cockpit. One witness recounted that he heard Burton say something like, "Someone needs to fly this plane." When the teenager returned to the rear, a group of passengers attempted to restrain him. For a while, the situation seemed defused, but as the plane was landing, it escalated again. The passengers mobilized. By the time the flight was at the gate, Burton was dying. He had been suffocated.

The simplest explanation, which seemed to satisfy authorities and the media, is that Burton went crazy and a larger disaster was narrowly averted. But Hunter, who knew a thing or two about crowd behavior, saw the episode from a different angle: a mob had gotten out of control.

THOMPSON: Interesting subjects are hard to come by. Here's one: a passenger on a plane was murdered, and now it's very hushed up. I am offended when that happens. Always. What interest me with this case is that I'm not quite sure what I would have done. I don't see any humor in freaks trying to break into the cockpit. But as a precedent, it's terrifying. It can't be passed off as normal. It gives airlines unholy leverage over all passengers. "Shut up or you'll be killed." This is something Nixon would do—have a passenger killed with no explanation. What time is it in Vegas?

STREITFELD: About 9:30 p.m.

THOMPSON: I want to call the mayor.

He called Oscar Goodman, the mayor of Vegas, plucking the number off a massive Rolodex. The phone rang and rang but Thompson finally succeeded in leaving a message.

THOMPSON: This story affects me personally. I don't plan to go to Jerusalem any time soon, but I do intend to fly Southwest Airlines.

He rummaged through his Rolodex again and found the name of a USA Today *reporter.*

THOMPSON: *[Into phone]* Hi, Mike. Hunter Thompson here. Looking into this killing of the passenger on the Southwest flight. It's a spooky story, but I understand you have some information. Can you give me a ring on that? *[Hangs up, brooding.]*

If I killed someone, I'd be hauled into a courtroom. I'd be up on homicide charges.

STREITFELD: While we're waiting for those calls to be returned, let's talk about your letters. You saved copies of every letter you wrote.

THOMPSON: I have something like twenty thousand of them. Writing letters may have been a way of working out the adrenaline of the day. People wrote me, I wrote them back, they wrote back. Like Kurt Vonnegut said, every time I answer a letter I get a pen pal.

[He had me read some of the letters aloud—asking visitors to read his work was a frequent Thompson gambit. He liked to hear the music in his words. I started with a June 21, 1973, letter to CBS correspondent Hughes Rudd: "I'm sitting out here in stone poverty—having taken a 'leave of absence' from [*Rolling Stone*] about three months ago—and juggling an outline for a novel (Jesus, what kind of a lunatic would try to sell anybody a novel at this foul stage in our history???) . . . It's been a weird night and I've been dealing with a head full of something rumored to be LSD-25 for the past six hours, but on the evidence I suspect it was mainly that PCP animal tranq, laced with enough speed to keep the arms & legs moving. The brain is another question, I think, but I keep hoping we'll have it under control before long . . . along with this goddamn rotten typewriter."]

THOMPSON: It's like the first draft of a life. I wasn't thinking of the letters as a document. But I am amazed at the sense of recording history. Somehow, I was in the middle of it, way too often for it to be accidental.

STREITFELD: For all the murderous history of those years, there was a sense of hope back then—tortured, stunted, but real. It was the dream of a better world. I feel that's mostly lacking now.

THOMPSON: The world apparently got the best of us.

Technology got the best of us. When in doubt, tighten up and continue on. Become a turtle.

STREITFELD: That's not what you do.

THOMPSON: I rely on my instincts. They've been pretty good over the years. They kept me alive.

STREITFELD: Jann Wenner once said you had the soul of an accountant.

THOMPSON: Fuck no.

STREITFELD: But there's something to the notion. You keep track of things. You saved carbons of all your letters. This house is a Hunter Thompson museum. The walls are covered with documents, the shelves with your books.

THOMPSON: I like to see what I've done. It's inspiration. Incentive. You can get into the habit of writing as easily as you can get into the habit of not writing. Once you get going, the trick is make yourself feel guilty for *not* working on the book.

STREITFELD: Are you working on a book?

THOMPSON: In answer to your question, "What the fuck are you doing these days?" I am deeply in the middle of selling out—which includes sending you down the fucking river—as part of my new deal with Al Gore. If he gets elected, you'd better watch out. Drug abuse is on the hit list.

[I read again from Fear and Loathing in America, *this time a 1971 memo detailing "Instructions for Reading Gonzo Journalism." It advocated taking a* "half-pint, 10-inch hypo-needle (the kind used for spinal taps & inoculating bulls)" and filling it "full of rum, tequila or Wild Turkey & shoot the entire contents straight into the stomach, thru the navel. This will induce a fantastic rush—much like a three-quarters-hour amyl high—plenty of time to read the whole saga."]

STREITFELD: You sat out this election, journalistically.

THOMPSON: I was hounded incessantly to cover it. I can't understand how Gore's botching it so incredibly. Clinton has a 70-percent approval rating. It's the finest economy in the history of man. And yet Gore's on the defensive.

STREITFELD: And yet . . .

THOMPSON: I'd be embarrassed to support either Gore or George Bush. *[He shrugged.]*

If Bush wins, life will pick up for me.

STREITFELD: You published a few years ago a little pamphlet on Timothy Leary, *Mistah Leary He Dead.* I brought it along. "I won't hear his laughing voice on my midnight telephone anymore," you write. "He believed, as I do, that 'after midnight, all things are possible.'"

THOMPSON: He conned me into doing it. I never liked him.

I was opposed to him from the start. Here's a guy who deliberately misled a whole generation. I knew he was a phony
and a fraud. He called me every night for the last two weeks
when he was dying, pleading forgiveness. Leary's story goes
to the heart of a whole generation. If I'd done what he did I'd
crucify myself.

STREITFELD: In the movie of *Fear and Loathing in Las
Vegas*, the Hunter character says that Leary "crashed around
America selling 'consciousness expansion' without ever giving
a thought to the grim meat-hook realities that were lying in
wait for all the people who took him seriously."

THOMPSON: It's grim, grim. He knowingly misled people
about what drugs could do. I've made some mistakes in my
time and I've been wrong but I never did that. I never made
drugs seem easy.

STREITFELD: So history will judge him harshly?

THOMPSON: History judges you for being dumb. I have seen
peaks and valleys. But there's no recourse for being dumb. This is
the age of the new dumb, a different kind of dumb. Rich dumb.

He took my copy of the Leary pamphlet and wrote on it, "Tim
Leary eats shit." *Then he resumed trying to get somewhere with
his Southwest story. He called Kent Spence, a lawyer for the dead
teen's family.*

[Into phone.] Hey Kent, Hunter Thompson here. Haven't

talked to you in a while, need some info. I may have gotten a little information myself. Give me a ring.

STREITFELD: Corporations have the upper hand these days.

THOMPSON: Everything's being blamed on the customer now. If airlines get the right to kill unruly passengers, what about Safeway and Walmart?

[He brooded, sketching out possible titles on a pad:

> "Las Vegas Redux—Fear and Loathing at 29,540 feet"
> "The Terrifying Story of a Passenger Stomped to
>   Death by Strangers"
> "Would You Buy a Seat from this Airline?"
> "Death Ship Out of Vegas"]

I can see all kinds of possibilities in this fucker. There's a great screenplay. Someone's going to suffer for the money. There will be charges. Trials. I kind of assume Spence is going to file a wrongful death suit. You find the weakest link and punch it.

STREITFELD: That could be your motto. Do you ever think about your legacy?

THOMPSON: I consider myself a Man of Letters. Letters cannot be rewritten and these haven't. Wenner wanted me to make a plea of temporary insanity before the fact—that I was out of my head when I wrote some of them. I'm finally getting paid for all the stuff I wrote back then. This is the triumph of a writer. No one's a writer who doesn't get paid.

STREITFELD: And your wild side?

THOMPSON: I was trapped in a persona to put bread on the table. If you don't put bread on the table you're a failure.

STREITFELD: In time, the letters might be seen as your best work.

THOMPSON: I've proved my point. Whatever my point was. I didn't mean to prove it. This is the bedrock of what really happened. Like a calendar. I didn't keep all these fuckers around because I wanted to publish them. I guess I thought they might be a valuable record.

STREITFELD: You're in the Modern Library now. You're practically an institution.

THOMPSON: If you're the mayor of Las Vegas in a hundred years, Las Vegas is going to be what I said. I wrote the book on Las Vegas. I did it.

STREITFELD: What's left to do?

THOMPSON: It's time I checked out. It's all said and done.

[The phone continues not to ring. None of his sources are coming through.]

STREITFELD: I might have to file my interview before you get to the bottom of this Southwest story.

THOMPSON: It's a deadline—you can miss it!

That was the last time I saw Hunter. He never published anything on the Southwest flight and its doomed passenger. He could not inject himself into the story, which always produced his best work. The third volume of his letters was announced several times but never appeared. There were rumors the quality did not hold up, the result of too many drugs for too many years.

"FEAR AND LOATHING AFTER 9/11"

INTERVIEW BY MICK O'REGAN
THE MEDIA REPORT
AUGUST 29, 2002

MICK O'REGAN: Hunter S. Thompson is a stirrer, a deliberately provocative commentator and a freewheeling iconoclast, infamous for his relentless critique of the American government and military. He lives in the Rocky Mountains of Colorado and that's where I found him at the end of a less-than-perfect telephone line. I wanted to ask his opinion of the state of the US media.

The first question is, how you would rate the American media in their coverage of the attack last September? What's your assessment of how the American media has performed?

HUNTER S. THOMPSON: Well, let's see, "shamefully" is a word that comes to mind. That's not true in the case of *The New York Times* and *The Washington Post*, but overall American journalism was cowed—cowed and intimidated by this massive flag-sucking, this patriotic orgy that the White House keeps whipping up. If you criticize the president it's unpatriotic and there's something wrong with you and you may be a terrorist. I've been raging against this from the very beginning, but I don't have much of a national platform because I've been working on this book, *Kingdom of Fear*, which probably describes what's been going on over here—it's a kingdom of fear.

O'REGAN: There's not enough room for dissenting voices?

THOMPSON: There's plenty of room. There's not just enough people who are willing to take the risk. It's sort of a herd mentality, a lemming-like mentality. If you don't go with the flow you're anti-American and therefore a suspect. We've seen this before, these patriotic frenzies in wartime. It's very convenient having an undeclared war that you can call a war and impose military tribunals and wartime security, and then we have these generals telling us that this war's going to go on for a long, long time. Maybe it's not so much the generals now, the generals are a little afraid of Iraq, a little worried about it, but it's the civilians in the White House, the gang of thieving lobbyists for the military-industrial complex who are running the White House. If it's patriotic to be against them, then hell, call me a traitor.

O'REGAN: Do you think that most of the influential American media has bought that patriotism line, and as a result are self-censoring themselves?

THOMPSON: Self-censorship, yes, that's a very good point. Yeah, I would say that. Now there are always exceptions, but there've been damn few. Maureen Dowd of *The New York Times* . . . I'm trying to think of who else. There's not that many of them that come to mind. And you get that corporate mentality of what will the advertisers think? A kind of we're all in this together thinking. The publishers have always been Republicans and the working press usually Democratic, the smarter part of them, but not even the Democrats have been very strong on this. Not strong enough to get anybody excited.

O'REGAN: So is the White House laying down what they think is appropriate journalism, or are the media outlets deciding that they have to be patriotic?

THOMPSON: It goes a little deeper than that, because this administration is well on the road to seizing power. Tom Daschle, the Senate Democratic leader, the other day accused Bush of trying to seize dictatorial powers. Now that was a big breakthrough, and I'm starting to sense that the tide may be turning against the president; we have to beat this bastard one way or another. And the easiest way to do it is vote. Just voting should be sufficient. I have a sense that there is some kind of flag of courage—courage to disagree with the government. And that's what this country is all about, really.

O'REGAN: Historically that's obviously hugely important for America.

THOMPSON: The American government is the greatest enemy of freedom around the world that I can think of. These people are flag-suckers.

O'REGAN: What about the language that's being used to describe the so-called undeclared war? There have been criticisms in the mainstream press in Australia that journalists have too readily taken up the language of politicians and bureaucrats, that they have uncritically declared a war against terror without really thinking it through. What's your assessment of the situation in the States?

THOMPSON: Well, I'm glad to hear that—you're talking about Australian journalists?

O'REGAN: Yes.

THOMPSON: Yes, well that's good. Congratulations, boys. There is not much of that in this country yet. *The New York Times*—the paper of record—has been I think pretty courageous in terms of just laying out what is going on. Reading *The New York Times* for the past year has been like one funeral dirge or just one funeral after another. This over here is the most paranoid, most insecure country that I've ever lived in, I mean it's the worst this country has been since I have ever seen it. And I've been covering politics for a long time.

O'REGAN: So that's how you'd characterize the popular debate at the moment? That it's full of paranoia?

THOMPSON: Soon, if you look at it just a little bit with a different prism, this could be a military takeover. It could be called that. Have you noticed all the power being centralized in the White House, in Washington? When these super agencies take over the FBI, the CIA, the super-cabinet positions? This little bastard of a president, the goofy child president—I used to call him that, but goofy is way too friendly for a president who's presiding over the looting of the treasury and the looting of people's pension funds. He's done a lot of damage. And he's trying to. His next step I guarantee is to overrule the Freedom of Information Act that is key to the survival of journalism in this country.

O'REGAN: Do you feel like there is a restricted space for media freedom?

THOMPSON: I wouldn't say it's a restricted space, but it's a dark and dangerous area to venture into. Several journalists have lost their jobs. Some people were made an example of early on. And then you have the argument, if you want to criticize like that you're making fun of the victims or people who died in the disaster.

There's a lot more to it that than we've been allowed to know over here. The media doesn't reflect world opinion or even a larger, more intelligent opinion over here, it's just this drumbeat of celebrity worship and child funerals and hooded prisoners being led around Guantanamo. I'm very disturbed about the civil rights implications of this. Everybody should be.

O'REGAN: Are you saying that journalists who came out and were fearless in their critique of the government or the government's policy actually lost their jobs?

THOMPSON: I can think of two that come to mind right in the beginning. I haven't heard of any since. Bill Maher [host of the ABC show *Politically Incorrect*] talked about how these dirty little bastards snuck up on us and pulled off what amounts to a perfect crime, no witnesses, very little cost; talk about cost-effective, that was a hell of a strike. He said he considered our missile attacks and our bombing attacks on unseen victims, wedding parties, etc.—*that* was cowardly. Whacko. A huge tidal wave of condemnation came down on him.

O'REGAN: So at the moment people don't want to hear that sort of criticism, they want people to rally round the flag and support the military?

THOMPSON: I think that's right, and I think the reason they don't want to hear it is because boy, that's going to be a lot of agonizing reappraisal. Popular opinion in this country has to be swung over to "the White House is wrong, these people are corporate thieves." They've turned the American Dream into a chamber of looting. It would take a lot of adjustment, mentally.

O'REGAN: At the moment, even in Australia, the media is preparing for the first anniversary of the attacks. Can you give me a sense of what is happening in the United States?

THOMPSON: You would never believe it, it's so insane. There is frantic publicity. The president's on TV at least once a day, and celebrations of the dead, the patriots, exposés on Al-Qaeda—it's just relentless, twenty-five hours a day of just how tragic it was and how patriotic it was, and how much we have to get back at these dirty little swine. As hideous and dumb as it sounds, I wouldn't be at all surprised by an invasion of Iraq on September 11. I'll take a long shot bet on that.

O'REGAN: You think that the anniversary might actually an appropriate day to launch an invasion?

THOMPSON: It seems like that to me, because that's their only power base, really—that frenzy of patriotism. It's our revenge strike. Uncle Sam gets even. If that's going to work at all, there would be no time when it would work better than when everyone in the country is cranked up into emotional frenzies. I found myself getting a little teary-eyed last night watching some CNN special. Anita [his wife] was crying. This reminds me exactly of the month after the attack when there was just one drumroll after another. But there is some opposition now popping up in this country, a lot of it. High-level opposition.

O'REGAN: I would like to come to the opposition in just a moment. But about the manipulation by the media of popular sentiments—what do you think the leading media outlets should be doing? Because obviously there is deep feeling within the American community about the attack and the aftermath of the attack, which the media is obviously going to pick up on. How do you represent that feeling without manipulating it for some other, less noble purpose?

THOMPSON: That grief has been manipulated here and turned into a platform for revenge, but on who? Osama bin Laden? First it was Osama, then it was Saddam Hussein. It may be that the secret police and the intelligence operations of America are so much smarter than we are and know so much more than we heard and are so much more responsible and effective than we are. That's possible, I suppose. In fact, though, all these agencies have been embarrassed. They've been proven to be buffoons and liars. Some FBI agent lost seven hundred guns in two years. These agencies are riddled with corruption and an unwillingness to challenge the word of authority. It's un-American to lean back and be a sheep and act like a good German.

O'REGAN: So you would say there's been a failure to challenge authority?

THOMPSON: There hasn't been much challenging of authority for quite a while. This president here, this little bastard, is just a creation of his father and the Reagan brain trust. A lot of those people came out of Nixon, it's really like the rebirth of Richard Nixon. Nixon lives! But these people make Nixon look like a liberal.

O'REGAN: You would argue that George Bush, Jr., makes Richard Nixon seem like a liberal—which is a startling admission from you because of the caustic way you have previously described Richard Nixon.

THOMPSON: Yeah, it shocked me when I said it. But I'll stick with that. In terms of just a mean, greedy, tunnel-visioned looter, these people make Nixon look like a statesman.

O'REGAN: Now Nixon, of course, was undone by the actions of two members of the press, Bernstein and Woodward, who doggedly pursued him even though it wasn't initially apparent that that trail would bear fruit. Is there a new generation of investigative journalist in the United States, and is this the moment that it should come forward?

THOMPSON: I've been looking for that—for the rise of that generation—for a long time. Nixon was always convinced there was a massive liberal conspiracy to get him. Well, he was right. I was part of that. And I'm proud of it.

O'REGAN: Now is that so-called massive liberal conspiracy emerging in the debate around the potential invasion of Iraq or the conduct of the Bush administration?

THOMPSON: No, these Jesus freaks have managed to give the word "liberal" such a bad name that now it's really a matter of shame to adopt the word. See, I've never been a liberal. But there's no groundswell of liberal sentiment driving this questioning of what the administration is doing. These people want to go attack the Arab world, the Muslim world, with no allies except England and Israel—

O'REGAN: And possibly Australia.

THOMPSON: Oh my God! Don't tell me you goddamned Papist bastards are that bad off. I thought you were freedom-loving *[inaudible]*?

O'REGAN: Well, as we record this interview in Australia, there is actually a debate about the degree to which the government has made clear whether it would support a first-strike policy by the United States. The call in Australia is for a much fuller debate both at a parliamentary level and in the media. The prime minister of Australia has reserved his judgment, but he's made it clear that his government is very keen to support the US if called upon.

THOMPSON: That's horrible. You're all subjects of the Queen, aren't you?

O'REGAN: We voted not to become a republic, that's right.

THOMPSON: No, no, you reaffirmed the power of the monarchy as I remember.

O'REGAN: It's a digression, but that's right. One of the things that the media in Australia is really trying to take up is to draw from the government some clearer position. You know, will Australia support the US, what are the implications of the US striking pre-emptively against Iraq? I'm very interested in your assessment of that debate in the States.

THOMPSON: Let me first say that it's very important that you guys get a statement, a clear statement, out of the government. And the longer they won't give you one, the more ominous it's going to sound, right? If they won't tell you they *won't* support the United States in the event of a first strike, what do you guess their position is going to be?

O'REGAN: In Australia, Hunter, there's been a history of bipartisanship, and that's the other thing that's up for grabs at the moment. The question is whether the Labour Party opposition to the Conservative federal government is going to strengthen its opposition to any Australian involvement, or whether it's going to go ahead and support the government, as it has in previous military campaigns. That's a major issue, but it's an issue being played out in the press. What I'm interested in is your assessment of how that's being played out or not being played out in your own press.

THOMPSON: Nobody is really in favor of this [invasion]. Who else really wants Saddam Hussein so desperately out of power? I look around, I don't see anyone else waving the hatchet, do you?

O'REGAN: Could I take you back to September 11? What I'd really like to know is your reactions. And I know you said you were writing a sports column for *ESPN* when the planes hit the towers, but could I get you to tell that story of when you found out about it and what you were doing and what your reaction was?

THOMPSON: I had in fact just finished a sports column for *ESPN*. I've forgotten exactly what it was about. It was pretty good. No sooner had it gone over the wire than I was on the phone with John Walsh, general editor of *ESPN*. He was saying, "You have to write about this disaster," and as it happened I was just going to bed. The TV was still on. I usually have it on just for the news, and I happened to see the first plane hit, and even in my foggy condition, I'd been up all night writing the column, I somehow knew it was real. I don't know why.

[Beeping sound]

What is that noise? Yeah, there was no mistaking the reality. It didn't make much sense. And it still doesn't really, but . . .

Here we go. This is the column I wrote, let's see, September 12, 2001: "It was just after dawn in Woody Creek, Colorado, when the first plane hit the World Trade Center in New York City on Tuesday morning, and as usual I was writing about sports. But not for long. Football suddenly seemed irrelevant compared to the scenes of destruction and utter devastation coming out of New York on TV."

O'REGAN: You went on to say in that article, which I have in front of me, that "even ESPN was broadcasting war news. It was the worst disaster in the history of the United States." Do you think that the event completely transformed the way in which Americans see themselves and their own vulnerability?

THOMPSON: No, the event by itself would not have done that. I've seen planes hit the Empire State Building before, I didn't go totally out of my mind. People have been killed before. But it was the way the administration was able to use that event as a springboard for everything they wanted to do. And that might tell you something. I remember when I was writing that column you sort of wonder when something like that happens, who stands to benefit? You know, it's like murder. Who had the opportunity and the motive? You have to look at these basic things. I don't know if I want to go into this on worldwide radio here, but—

O'REGAN: You may as well.

THOMPSON: All right. I saw that the US government was

going to benefit, and the White House people, the Republican administration, to take the mind of the public off of the crashing economy. You want to keep in mind that every time a person named Bush gets into office, the nation goes into a drastic recession.

O'REGAN: It sounds almost like the plot of that film *Wag the Dog*, where film producers concocted a national event to inspire patriotism to take the public's minds off misdemeanors committed by the president. Are you suggesting that this worked in the favor of the Bush Administration?

THOMPSON: Absolutely. And I have spent enough time on the inside of, well, in the White House and campaigns and I've known enough people who do these things and think this way to know that the public version of the news or whatever event is never really what happened. And the [Bush] people I think are willing to take that even further. I don't assume that I know the truth of what went on that day. I am just looking around for who had the motive, who had the opportunity, who had the equipment, who had the will. These people were looting the treasury and they knew the economy was going into a spiral downward.

O'REGAN: From this distance it does seem extraordinarily conspiratorial that you could sit there and see the hand of the US government in this attack, rather than seeing international terrorists bent on somehow hurting America and the American people. What sort of reaction did your views get among your peers or among other journalists?

THOMPSON: [*Laughs*] I was greeted universally with a kind of nervousness. Almost nobody agreed with me, nobody thought it was the right thing. It was about ninety-nine-to-one [against me], but since then—

O'REGAN: Did you publish those views anywhere?

THOMPSON: If I haven't, then I meant to. Now, let's see—

O'REGAN: I was going to ask you for the reaction to them because it does seem an extraordinary conspiracy theory that you're putting forward. Your first reaction was somehow to implicate the US government in this attack, rather than an enemy of the US government.

THOMPSON: You'll want to keep in mind that I have been very close to a lot of real tragedies in this country. Let me ask you, do you think you know who killed John Kennedy or Robert Kennedy?

O'REGAN: I was a boy at the time, but no, and I haven't read the Warren Commission report. But it seems to me that that in this case there would have to have been so many more people involved it would seem much less likely to be some sort of conspiracy.

THOMPSON: Well, it does. I can see why you are a little edgy accepting this from me and—

O'REGAN: You've pioneered a form of journalism called

Gonzo, in which there's no revision. What you see and feel is what goes down on the page, and it's that first blush, that first image, that hits the readership. Does that mean that it's hard for you to appear credible within the US media because people would say, "Oh look, that's just another conspiracy theory from drug-addled Gonzo journalist Hunter S. Thompson"?

THOMPSON: Yeah, that's a problem. I'm not sure if it's my problem or other people's, but I'm looking at this [September 11] column and the one after it—I've been right so often, and my percentages are so high, I'll stand by this column that I wrote that day, and the next one. I'm not going to claim any prophetic powers, but—

O'REGAN: One of the things you do say in that first article you wrote is, "It is twenty-four hours later now, and we are not getting much information about the Five Ws of this thing." Now by the Five Ws I'm presuming you mean the Who, the What, the When, the Why, and the How. Is that still how you feel, that a year later those key questions haven't been answered?

THOMPSON: Absolutely. It's even worse, though. This was just a suggestion in twenty-four hours we were not getting much information about the Five Ws. Well, how much have we got beyond that? How much more do we have than we had a year ago? Damn little, I think. We know a lot about the firemen who died, a lot about the people who stole money from their charity fund, a lot about the people who donated all that blood, and the Red Cross had too much of it and had to throw away five tons of blood or something like that. That may be an exaggeration. *[Begins to ramble.]* No, I will stand by almost all my . . . well no, no, come on, look, get a grip on yourself, you can't talk like that . . .

O'REGAN: Let me ask you about your new book, *Kingdom of Fear: Loathsome Secrets of a Star-Crossed Child in the Final Days of the American Century.* It's a very apocalyptic title. Has this new book come off your reflections about September 11 and the way it was handled by the American media?

THOMPSON: It came off the atmosphere in this country as of September 12. Yeah, *Kingdom of Fear.* That's the way I see this country. I'm not just writing a long screed front-to-back, some kind of a political tract. I've tried to explain a little bit about how I got this way and why you should pay attention to my predictions.

O'REGAN: Is this a critical time for the credibility of US journalism?

THOMPSON: I think definitely, but I'm not sure how much credibility US journalism really has. Let's see, in five years we lost two presidents [unclear what Thompson means here] and one civil rights leader to mysterious bombs and assassins, bushy-haired strangers, and US journalism has never dug out the truth about that. One of my great shames as a journalist is that I still don't know who killed Jack Kennedy.

It's always bothered me, it's always haunted me. There's no doubt that I don't know, and that journalism in general does not know. And in a lot of ways, that may be because we haven't asked. Most of the witnesses were killed, weren't they?

O'REGAN: That need for certainty—is that what underpins your critique that US journalism has failed to provide the key answers to the key events?

THOMPSON: I would say that, and I would include myself, and I worked as hard as anybody. The rules really changed in this country when Reagan came in and started these test invasions of small nations. Then they decided to test the policy of no more battlefield access for any journalist. Vietnam was totally different and that's why we got that war ended. I went to Grenada [after the US military invaded the Caribbean island in 1983] and that's in this book too. I had never seen journalists beaten up by military police and hogtied in the middle of the road. I always had a press pass and access. But when the military seized the advantage, they never gave it up. The military is still not allowing anybody else to know what's happening in Afghanistan or wherever they're fighting. It's always press releases, staged events.

O'REGAN: Do you think that the so-called Gonzo style of journalism for which you've become famous—and, some would say, notorious—has a specific legacy that makes it more necessary at the moment?

THOMPSON: Well, I've never properly defined that term even to myself.

O'REGAN: What do you think it means?

THOMPSON: From my point of view it means being very skeptical of the pronouncements of authority. As a gambler I would say that it is a bit of an even bet that if you question the statements and truths of the White House and the government, more often than not you'll be right.

I just try to get as close to what I'm writing about as possible in order to find out what's really happening. A lot of times it is weirder than it appears in my stories. The truth is usually stranger than fiction, in my life.

O'REGAN: Will you be watching the commemoration programs on the eleventh of September? Will you be among the audience, which I imagine will number tens of millions of people, who watch what happens in New York?

THOMPSON: That's a good question. It's soon, isn't it? No, I won't. I think I'll grab Anita and take a road trip. We'll just go off and have a little fun. Why sit around and watch that stuff? Now what I'm afraid of is that's going to a cover for a sudden move on Iraq. And that little monster will come on TV and say, "Today the . . ." Well, he can't say "allied forces," he can't say "coalition forces" anymore, he'll have to say, "Today we invaded Iraq." Now, this seems so impossible I'd be happy to lose money on it. But I'd bet on it. It seems too logical for that kind of tactless thug mindset not to do it.

I can't think of a better time if I was going to do it, I'll put it that way.

O'REGAN: It's almost like saying, "Quick, while no one's really paying attention, let's invade another country."

THOMPSON: Exactly. It's so cynical, and so stupid, and so self-defeating in the long run that you'd think that nobody in their right mind—no president—would plunge us into a war like that with no allies and [the battleground] on the other side of the world.

O'REGAN: These comments will be broadcast on Radio National in Australia, which is part of the public broadcasting network. It occurs to me that you probably wouldn't hear those sort of comments on other outlets.

THOMPSON: Well, I definitely will be [making those comments] when this book comes out in December. Now, unfortunately, we're going to have that election up here in November. And that is going to be an extremely key election if you care about this country.

O'REGAN: So, obviously these very critical views will appear in your book. I suppose what I'm asking is, where else would people hear views like yours? I know they will be out later in the year in your book, but across the US media, radio, and television and print, where would people hear very critical comments such as the ones you've been making?

THOMPSON: Where indeed? I know a lot of journalists across the country that would agree with me. But whether they are writing this stuff and saying it in public I don't know. You can ask Maureen Dowd and see if she feels if I'm right or wrong. I can't really tell you anybody else. Doesn't come to mind. Boy, it really is lonely out here.

O'REGAN: A final question is a big one, but let me ask it anyway. From your position as a critic on the left, how do you see the future of journalism in your country?

THOMPSON: I have a very dim view of it, I guess. I really thought the future of journalism was unbounded after Watergate but right now there's not a hell of a lot of reasons to be optimistic about it. Not because of the one huge scam they pulled off here, but because of the everyday reality of journalism is celebrity driven. The news over here is barely covered. I watched some BBC stuff and then some CNN foreign news—the world news that doesn't get into this country. I read the *Paris Herald Tribune [International Herald Tribune]*. That kind of news doesn't get through in this country. But I don't think my views would be seen as crazy or absurd or out of the question in most countries of the world.

O'REGAN: Do you ever worry, given the current climate in the United States and the surge in patriotism that's going on, that you could be personally at risk from someone who took offense at your critique?

THOMPSON: I think about it. Definitely could be true.

O'REGAN: Have there been occurrences when you've been threatened?

THOMPSON: Oh yeah. Constantly. I have been all my life. Yeah. With my kind of journalism, that goes with the territory. There are going to be threats, and there are going to be people who are very unhappy. And—knock, knock—I don't think it is a matter of luck [that nothing has happened], I think it's that I've pretty well stuck to my battle plan. They've tried to come after me—the federal government, all kinds of governments. I've got tons of warrants. I have to keep four of the finest criminal lawyers in the country on retainer. You have to fight for these rights in this country. The stork didn't bring a bill of rights. A lot of people fought for it.

O'REGAN: So that's how you'd see yourself—as fighting for freedom of speech in America?

THOMPSON: Absolutely.

THE LAST INTERVIEW "A DOWNHILL, HELLBOUND TRAIN"

INTERVIEW BY JESSICA HOPSICKER
THE COLLEGE CRIER
OCTOBER, 2004

JESSICA HOPSICKER: Hello.

HUNTER S. THOMPSON: All right, I'll move over here now, two outs at the bottom of the ninth here, the Yankees are behind, no runners on base, Boston's about to win. Ah, where am I, what phone am I talking on?
    Jessica?

HOPSICKER: Hello. Good evening.

THOMPSON: I'm sorry to keep you waiting. Life gets confusing around here.

HOPSICKER: That's all right. I was just about to finish up a beer and leave.

THOMPSON: Where are you?

HOPSICKER: I'm at the office right now.

THOMPSON: Where is the office?

HOPSICKER: In Barneveld, in upstate New York.

ANITA THOMPSON, HUNTER'S WIFE: Where do you go to school?

HOPSICKER: I went to Pratt Institute, in Brooklyn.

THOMPSON: The art school. Isn't it?

HOPSICKER: Oh, yeah. Studied graphic design for a bit, then decided it wasn't for me and decided to get my foot in the door for journalism, and somehow I found myself thrust headlong into it.

THOMPSON: How long have you been at it?

HOPSICKER: I did take a couple of journalism classes in Brooklyn, very interesting. Got into the politics of Brooklyn. But I never thought I'd be doing this.

THOMPSON: Well, what the hell? Why not? I got one of the few things I could do well and get paid for. Also, I got to go to work at two in the afternoon. That was what got me into journalism. You work for a morning paper and you work at night. So once I got a job there and could go to work at two in the afternoon, I never again had a nine-to-five job. That's why I'm a journalist.

HOPSICKER: That's part of the reason I was thinking about going into the business, too.

THOMPSON: Are you a night person?

HOPSICKER: I can be, every once in awhile.

ANITA THOMPSON: You are tonight.

THOMPSON: Well, it helps. Fire a question at me, and let's see if I can handle it.

HOPSICKER: After a recent round of censorship, a staffer at a certain sports media outlet was quoted as saying, "Hunter had gone too far."

THOMPSON: You talk to people on the phone, you've got to learn to slow down and bite your words off. I know I talk fast, but I'm a good voice critic of other people.

HOPSICKER: I'm also a bit nervous, too.

THOMPSON: Oh, don't worry about it.

ANITA THOMPSON: You're doing fine.

THOMPSON: Do you have any drugs? Do you have any drugs with you?

HOPSICKER: Not with me, just a bunch of beer and cigarettes.

THOMPSON: Well, that won't really work, I'll smoke some pot for you here. It is a nice kind of deep orange and almost turquoise California weed. That should calm you down, you'll get a contact buzz.

HOPSICKER: Yeah, that'll work.

THOMPSON: Feeling any better? I'm getting a little stoned now, so you should start to feel it soon. How old are you?

HOPSICKER: I'm twenty-one.

THOMPSON: Twenty-one, and you've already been through design? That's pretty good. I have a design background.

HOPSICKER: Really?

THOMPSON: Yeah, photography. Taschen Books is publishing a book of my photographs. You know that high-end publishing company in Beverly Hills? They produce very beautiful books. I mean the best in the business, no doubt. They produced that Muhammad Ali book that weighs eighty-five pounds. It's called *GOAT: Greatest of All Time*. I think it costs eight thousand dollars or something like that. I have an old interview; a piece I did on Muhammad Ali. It's in there; it's one of the essays in the book. It's beautiful. If you ever get a chance to see *GOAT*, it's *Greatest of All Time*. It's really a museum piece. It's wonderful. Like the heaviest, the highest reach in book publishing in American history. It's the largest book ever published. Takes two people to carry it.

All right, where's that pipe now? Ah, here we go. Little mechanical problem like they have at the air flights. Er, airports. I'm getting nervous myself. All right, I feel better now. I hope you do.

HOPSICKER: Contact buzz.

THOMPSON: Right. But what you mentioned about censorship there, what was that?

HOPSICKER: A staffer at a certain major media outlet was recently quoted as saying, "Hunter can go too far at times."

THOMPSON: Too far? Well, that's what it's about. If you never go too far, you never have any real sense of adventure. What's too far? That's a matter of taste. Yeah, I believe that's true. Too far is a matter of personal choice. I'm a very down-to-earth person. I'm a neighborhood pillar of strength. I've lived in the same house here for thirty years. So I'm not really as weird as you may have heard. Are you hearing weird things about me? Why are you doing this, how did you get this assignment?

HOPSICKER: Well, my sister is a bowling alley waitress. She talked to a local newspaper and said that I wanted to get into journalism. I mentioned that I enjoy reading your work and the next thing I know, here I am, on the phone with you.

THOMPSON: Damn, that's fast work.

HOPSICKER: Yeah. Thrust headlong into journalism.

THOMPSON: Yep, that's right. Yeah, you were. Well, I'd like to send you some reading material. I'd like to advance your career if I could. It makes me feel good to communicate with my tribe. I'm a journalist. And I write novels, and I write . . . what don't I do? I'm a photographer. But right now I'm a political journalist. Have you seen my column in the online *ESPN* this week?

HOPSICKER: Yeah.

ANITA THOMPSON: The book?

THOMPSON: What book?

ANITA THOMPSON: The book.

THOMPSON: Oh, *Hey Rube*, that's what we're talking about.

HOPSICKER: I have yet to read that.

THOMPSON: It's a must. First, it's a lot of fun. You don't have to be a sports fan to read this. It is a really brutal political book.

ANITA THOMPSON: It's *Hey Rube: Blood Sport, the Bush Doctrine and the Downward Spiral of Dumbness, Modern History From the Sports Desk.* It's the unedited version of his *ESPN* online column.

THOMPSON: I write a sports column every week. Is that right? Jessica, you've got to get a little drunk. So what are you most curious about?

HOPSICKER: I'm just curious about everything right now. Trying to expand my horizons.

THOMPSON: What's your job assignment?

HOPSICKER: Just to interview you right now.

THOMPSON: And get an interview that you can fit on black and white paper and print. Is that right?

HOPSICKER: Yup, and on the website.

THOMPSON: In any case, we will see it in print, somewhere, somehow.

HOPSICKER: Yup.

THOMPSON: Are you a runaway child, Jessica?

HOPSICKER: Nope, small-town girl, born and raised.

THOMPSON: What town was that again?

HOPSICKER: I grew up in Hinckley, a very small town in the foothills of the Adirondack Mountains.

THOMPSON: You're a hillbilly! I am too.

HOPSICKER: It's a good life.

THOMPSON: Hmm, what can I teach Jessica here? My beautiful wife is going to explain the setup for you. It will give you a lead for your piece.

ANITA THOMPSON: What are we talking about?

THOMPSON: *Hey Rube,* I guess. I've written two books pounding George Bush mercilessly.

ANITA THOMPSON: They call it *The Journal of the Bush Presidency.* He's been writing this book since the very beginning of the election in 2000, and he chronicles all the chaos that was going on during the election and throughout the whole Bush presidency. And it's a journal that he wrote at the time, as it was happening. Very similar to *Campaign Trail.* It's not in retrospect.

THOMPSON: A good diary of the Bush presidency, a downhill, hell-bound train.

ANITA THOMPSON: And he also teaches you to gamble, and how not to gamble.

THOMPSON: And to shoot. I think we should set up to teach you shooting.

ANITA THOMPSON: Yeah. Hunter's property here is also the Woody Creek Rod and Gun Club.

THOMPSON: Which has many distinguished members.

ANITA THOMPSON: We called it the Woody Creek Rod and Gun Club after having a barbecue with the neighbors. One of the neighbors was running for county commissioner. So Hunter is actually as involved in local politics as he is in national politics.

THOMPSON: It's very important. That's what the Republicans did, in fact. They organized from the ground up, starting when Pat Robertson ran for president [in 1988]. He got beaten. He was an evangelical preacher in Virginia who runs the Christian Coalition. His party wasn't organized efficiently enough for him to win. I think he won Michigan—some terrifying blunder on everybody's part. He became a serious threat, like Ross Perot in '92. He'd gone from a local boy to a national boy, but he didn't have an organization in place, so he couldn't move from Michigan, for instance, to New York, for the primary. He'd have to get a whole new organization and teach them all over again. So he figured out that if you organize from the ground up, through his churches, that would give him a base in any city or state and he wouldn't have to teach them the ropes all over again. That's when the Republicans began their Christian jihad: the crusade. And it's still going on. Bush is a jackass, really. Incompetent, he's an imbecile. I looked up "imbecile" in *Black's Law Dictionary.*

An imbecile, under law, well, I can't remember it but it fits George Bush perfectly. It's an intelligence that never develops past sixteen or something like that. It's not a mental disease, therefore you can't hide behind it with an insanity defense. You can't plead insanity and not be executed for murder. But "imbecile" is just a slow-witted half-right yo-yo who is not really sick and can't be cured. You can't cure dumbness. But you can use it. And he got a job as, like, a male model. He was a perfect face for what the religious right and the power-mongers wanted. It is like going out and selling Ivory Snow, or like being a Chanel girl, except this is for the presidency. That's ridiculous. You have to like the president or be charmed by him or want to go out and have a drink, get naked with him. If you had to make a choice between getting naked with George Bush or John Kerry, who would you choose?

HOPSICKER: I'm not quite sure yet.

THOMPSON: Oh, don't give me that crap, Miss Undecided. What if you had to do it right now? See, this is training, Jessica. You have to make a decision right now.

HOPSICKER: Kerry?

THOMPSON: Kerry, I'm not gonna push you on this, but I'm curious as to why you'd rather get naked—

HOPSICKER: —than vote.

THOMPSON: Yeah, that really has nothing to do with it. But it does, in this country. I don't know what that means for the fact the women's vote is swinging to Bush. I don't know, I'm just jabbering. Ask me a question, Jessica.

Why am I hearing all this noise?

ANITA THOMPSON: Taking a message, *Rolling Stone* called.

THOMPSON: I'm writing a piece for *Rolling Stone* and I'm trying to talk to the editor about the piece.

HOPSICKER: Does journalistic objectivity still exist?

THOMPSON: Only in closed-circuit TV camera systems that observe everything that goes on in front of them all the time. You have to be a machine to be objective. Being objective really mandates that you miss a few things. You couldn't see Richard Nixon, for instance, being objective about him. Objectivity is good when you're learning journalism because you have to learn the Five Ws. You know about the Five W's?

HOPSICKER: The who, what, where, when, why?

THOMPSON: Exactly. Who, what, where, when, the other one's a tricky one. Why, or—

HOPSICKER: Sometimes how.

THOMPSON: Yeah, Numer Five is tricky. Why is the difference between objective and subjective journalism. Why is an interpretive concept. Where is not. You know, it happened at an address. I was an objective journalist for most of the time when I was learning it. I wrote for fifteen years before I published a book, which is a kind of measure of success in writing journalism. I think I've published fourteen [books]. But you have to learn. In order to play football, there are certain rules. Mainly it's about getting hired, getting a job. But journalism to me was always a fallback position. And I needed money so I had to agree to work on jobs. My job was to do what the editor wanted. That's how I learned. The editor would pay money. You'd get a check for doing what the editor wanted. But you usually wouldn't get checks for doing just what you wanted. It's a school of hard knocks. Does this make any sense to you, Jessica?

HOPSICKER: Oh yeah.

THOMPSON: So, what have you learned so far? Wait, who are you going to vote for?

HOPSICKER: I'm thinking along the lines of Kerry. He seems like the lesser of two evils.

THOMPSON: Yeah. In this case, he's a lot lesser. I'm gonna vote for Kerry. I worry, I constantly bitch at him for not being more aggressive and simply more fun. There's no doubt in my mind that Kerry would be a good president and extremely different from Bush, but the main thing is that Bush is not just a likeable cowboy, some "aw shucks" person, a man of good will, a compassionate conservative.

No. He's a front man for a gigantic combine of religious zealots and oil billionaires. Voting against Bush is to stop an approaching iceberg or glacier. Bush is taking over, the Bush people. You can't say it's just Bush. But he is a good, friendly front man, and meanwhile the machine keeps going. People keep getting poorer, losing more jobs, more health insurance, more pension funds. Bush has destroyed the economy in this country. But he has not destroyed the economy of Halliburton, the oil company that Dick Cheney was president of before he became vice president of the US. He was CEO. Anyway, you've got a choice of personalities here. I seem to be wandering further and further.

HOPSICKER: It's all right.

THOMPSON: I'm way beyond objective journalism, although I had to learn to be an objective journalist before I could be subjective. And the trick about being subjective is that you have to be employed to do it. Otherwise you're just some kind of silly poet out in the woods. I'm a professional journalist, and a writer. Yeah, it's a job for me. That's the way it should be for you.

HOPSICKER: What draws you to a subject to write about?

THOMPSON: Wow, good question. It's very broad, but it happens to be good. Well, this presidential election is one. Have you read *Vanity Fair* recently?

HOPSICKER: No, I haven't yet.

THOMPSON: That's an assignment. The assignment is, you should read the June issue.

ANITA THOMPSON: It has Brad Pitt on the cover.

THOMPSON: Yeah, the June issue of this year, from a couple of months ago, of *Vanity Fair*, because, well, Brad Pitt's on the cover. Yeah, I'd love you to read about Brad Pitt. No, I have a big story in there, and I was drawn to it. It's about—well, it's too complicated to explain to you, but it's about a young girl who's in prison in Colorado for a crime she did not and could not have committed. We're about to get her out of prison. I have a very political approach.

ANITA THOMPSON: Lisl.com.

THOMPSON: Yeah, write that down, Jessica, L-I-S-L dot com. The case right now is before the Colorado Supreme Court, and we're awaiting a decision. It's a major case.*

[Pause]

Did she leave?

ANITA THOMPSON: Are you there?

---

*Lisl Auman was a young woman who was sentenced to life in prison for felony murder of a police officer. Her accomplice had fired the fatal shot; at the time, Auman was already handcuffed in the back of police car. In 2005, the Colorado Supreme Court overturned Auman's conviction.

THOMPSON: Jessica, are you writing? Jessica?

HOPSICKER: Sorry about that.

THOMPSON: What happened?

HOPSICKER: I was looking for a pen and the next thing you know, I had accidentally pressed the talk button.

THOMPSON: Oh boy, Jessica, you really are starting from the beginning here. Do you write pages?

HOPSICKER: Um, just journalism assignments in school, and stuff like that.

THOMPSON: Yeah, but do you write stories?

HOPSICKER: I do.

THOMPSON: Good. Well, why don't you read one of them? No, never mind. This is like teaching a course.

Now, I approach stories that interest me for reasons beyond simple journalism, like, *oh this would be a good story because it involves the murder of a pregnant mother under treacherous circumstances.* Like you see them on the news, the Scott Peterson case. No, those things don't interest me. But things that have meaning interest me. Like cracking the criminal justice system in Denver. I didn't really go into this case with the idea of doing that. I took the case before I planned to write the story about it, so it worked out. I would have had to write the story once I got into it anyway. It happens that when I wrote that in *Vanity Fair*, it crystallized the whole story and all the details. We did a lot of research on it. That's a key aspect of journalism. We've taken that girl from total doom underneath the Colorado state women's prison to right on the verge of having her released.

This Bush-Cheney machine in the White House is the most dangerous situation I've ever seen the country in. The country is in worse shape today than I've ever ever seen it in, and it happened so fast. If Richard Nixon were running against George Bush today, I think I'd vote for Nixon.

HOPSICKER: Really?

THOMPSON: Yeah. I never thought I'd say that.

HOPSICKER: What do you feel would happen if Bush were reelected?

THOMPSON: More of the same of what's happening now. Namely, a looting of the federal treasury. This country has gone from being a prosperous nation at peace and now, four years later, we're a broke nation at war. That's a huge turnaround; the effect of a failing economy, although the war-making machine is doing better than ever. Corporate profits for defense companies, companies that make airplanes and security devices and machine guns. Their profits are up 200 percent over the year before. This is like the tryout period for Bush. I don't think he's going to win. But if he does get reelected [you can see the direction they're going in]. One of them is putting oil rigs in Colorado now, in the national parks, giving away the national parks to mining companies.

HOPSICKER: I've read the same thing about them mining in Alaska, too.

THOMPSON: Drilling for oil in the North Shore, that's one of them. And they're doing that. I think it was stopped for a while. Putting oil derricks and pipelines everywhere. It's sucking the energy out of the Earth. And it will run out in about thirty-seven years, according to the scientists who measure stuff like that. The price of a gallon of gas has gone—

ANITA THOMPSON: Jessica, do you know how much gas was in 2000?

THOMPSON: What do you pay now for gasoline?

HOPSICKER: Well, up in the Adirondacks it's about $2.09.

THOMPSON: And what was it when you got your driver's license, do you remember?

HOPSICKER: Probably around $1.50 or something. Way back when I was around sixteen.

THOMPSON: Well, now it's over three dollars out here. It's going to be five dollars. That's what it costs in France or even

England to buy gasoline. But that's sort of like the last gasoline that will be available, ever, because we're running out of oil. Shit, we're running out of national forests and open land. We're running out of jobs.

ANITA THOMPSON: It doesn't just affect the price of gasoline in your car, it affects products. Products have to be transported, mainly by semis, [and then there's] house heating. Rent prices go up. Jet fuel is based on the price of crude oil.

THOMPSON: All the premier airlines are filing for bankruptcy because of the price of fuel. I think the country is headed into the dark ages, and George Bush will be seen in history as the Adolf Hitler of his time. History will show that they committed war crimes worse than Hitler. They'll be put on trial eventually, and they'll be judged. Those religious freaks, let's see how they feel, being judged. Are you religious?

HOPSICKER: I don't really know yet. I've been spoon-fed a lot of religions, so I'm trying to weed some of it out.

THOMPSON: Have you tried Muslim? No, no. One thing that I was about to write here in my own article is, what kind of maniac would declare war on the rest of the world, turning the country into, yeah, like Nazi Germany. People aren't choosing to make the US a bunch of fascist Nazis, but the proof of it keeps coming. We invade countries, and then we wonder why they bitch and try to get back at us through terrorism. The Bush people have created this terrorism, this fear. I have a whole book, remember it? *Kingdom of Fear?*

HOPSICKER: I want to read that.

THOMPSON: You should. *Kingdom of Fear* and *Hey Rube* are going to be part of your permanent education. These are two books that are extremely political. Not just that, but if you're going to get into journalism, these are going to be some of your basic texts. What haven't I answered here? What haven't I said? I feel like I'm doing the interview.

HOPSICKER: What would you consider the foulest lie on the campaign trail of 2004?

THOMPSON: The foulest lie, I believe, is the one that says Bush is going to be a successful president and should be reelected again. That's absolutely 180 degrees off from the truth. He has been a disaster as president for the country. He's been a good boy for Halliburton, the oil industry. That's what he does, that's where he grew up. He grew up in the Petroleum Club of Houston, which is a huge power center of oil people. That's what he does. But it's not good for the country. What did Clinton do? He got a few blowjobs, and these goddamn religious zealots almost impeached him for it. Then they come in and steal five trillion dollars from the national treasury in the name of war on the rest of the world. What the fuck is that?

The lie is really that Bush, Cheney, et cetera, don't deserve to be fired and put in jail. They do. How would they run for president again and get reelected is almost beyond my ability to comprehend. The question now is not whether George Bush is a Nazi or whether John Kerry bled real blood in Vietnam or lied. That's all bullshit, all politics. That's just the presidential year. The question now is whether the American people, the voters, want it that way. Whether we as a democracy approve of having a failed preacher of the oil industry in charge of the country for another four years. I'd be a better drug czar than George Bush would be running the country.

You think George is stupid? The first time I saw George Bush, I met him, he came into my hotel room in Houston and passed out in the bathtub. Try that for a story. He was drunk. He was not invited, he came into the room with some friend of his who was invited, and he disappeared for a while. The next time I saw him, he was passed out in the bathtub and he had vomited on his seersucker suit. Yeah, that's a good image. But I've done worse things than that. I've done terrifying things under the influence of a variety of substances. But, to me, that's the most interesting thing he's done as a human being.

The weirdest thing that I've found in this election is that the women's vote is shifting to Bush. The women's vote has been strongly for Kerry in all the polls and predictions. About sixty-forty. But now, in the last two weeks, Bush has swept up about ten points in popularity among female registered voters. And that's the weirdest thing I've ever seen. I'd be afraid to get naked with George Bush. I mean, he's not a monster; he's just a nerd. Yeah, a nerd. He's like a drunken teenage kid.

HOPSICKER: It seems like voter apathy is prevalent today among college students.

THOMPSON: I've worried about that for so long. That's a silly excuse for not voting. You live in a country and bad things are happening to it, therefore to you. And you have a chance. This will be our last chance, really, for another four years, to kick the bastard out of the White House, to fire him. Not to vote is criminal and stupid, criminally stupid. It's the last time this oil machine is going to be stopped in our lifetime.

ANITA THOMPSON: The last page of *Hey Rube* is a tear-out of how important it is to vote.

THOMPSON: You have to read something, Jessica. Do you have access to a copy of *Hey Rube*?

HOPSICKER: I will get a copy of it.

THOMPSON: Read the last page first. You talk about apathy, well, apathy is what got us George Bush. Politics is such a vicious business when you're running for president. It's the most powerful job on Earth. Maybe not for long, but it is right now. And people will kill without even catching a breath. That's what you do in politics, you eliminate people. I've been in politics, writing about it, being in it, running for office, for forty years and I don't have any sure cure. It's like having the Hells Angels move into your house and having to kick them out. It's kind of hard to kick them out. Here's our chance, and to be apathetic about it is just stupid. It's self-destructive because the apathetic, the dumb, the floaters, are going to be eliminated immediately. There will be a massive crackdown on sex in public. Sex anywhere, really. I've always viewed Election Day as fun. I've always associated it with a kind of action. Pretty girls, getting laid, just fun. The thing to do this year is to get a date right now for Election Day. Be sure you have a date to vote with.

ANITA THOMPSON: Yeah, bring a date, have some fun.

THOMPSON: Hook up with somebody and vote.

ANITA THOMPSON: What do you think, Jessica? Think that's good?

HOPSICKER: I think it's a good idea.

THOMPSON: You have to make politics fun if you're going to run for office. It has to be fun for people or you won't get elected. It can only be a job for so long and then if it's not fun, you're not going to win. People won't come out and actually vote for you, they'll tell people they will. I think we need some fun in this campaign. I don't think there are any laws against voting naked while you're with a date. That sounds pretty good. Or you don't have to be naked to vote, but get naked afterwards. Yeah, wear an overcoat or trench coat to vote. I don't know what the hell I'm saying. I'd like to see what you write about this, Jessica. I want to see it. All this talk about politics is getting me excited.

HUNTER S. THOMPSON (1937-2005) was the inventor and pretty much the sole practitioner of Gonzo journalism. His first book, *Hell's Angels*, is the definitive work on the motorcycle gang. Gonzo was born with the 1970 magazine article, "The Kentucky Derby Is Decadent and Depraved," and reached a peak with *Fear and Loathing in Las Vegas*. His reporting on the 1972 campaign trail earned him accolades for being unafraid to tell the wretched truth about politics. On the basis of those pioneering works, Thompson became a celebrity and lived a life of wild abandon. When he killed himself, he left a note that read, "No more fun."

LOUIS "STUDS" TERKEL was a radio broadcaster and historian, known especially for his oral histories on topics including World War II, the Depression, race, jazz, and labor. He won the Pulitzer Prize in 1985 for *The Good War*. He died in 2008.

HENRY ALLEN is a poet, novelist, and artist. From 1970 to 2009, he was a staff writer at *The Washington Post*. He won a Pulitzer Prize for criticism in 2000. His latest book is *Where We Lived: Essays on Places*.

JANE PERLEZ is a longtime foreign correspondent for *The*

New York Times. She is currently the Beijing bureau chief. Before that, she served as bureau chief in Kenya, Poland, Austria, Indonesia, and Pakistan. She was a member of the team that won the Pulitzer Prize in 2009 for reporting in Pakistan and Afghanistan.

CURTIS WILKIE was a national and foreign correspondent for *The Boston Globe* for twenty-six years. He now teaches journalism at his alma mater, the University of Mississippi.

WILLIAM MCKEEN has written two books on Hunter Thompson: a volume in the Twayne academic studies series and a full-scale biography called *Outlaw Journalist*. He is chairman of the Department of Journalism at Boston University.

DAVID STREITFELD is the editor of *The Last Interview* books on Gabriel Garcia Marquez, Philip K. Dick, and J. D. Salinger, all published by Melville House. He is a reporter for *The New York Times*, where in 2013 he was part of the team awarded the Pulitzer Prize for Explanatory Reporting. He lives in the San Francisco Bay Area with his family and too many books.

MICK O'REGAN is an Australian journalist and broadcaster who has worked for public and commercial media for thirty years. His interest in Hunter Thompson began in the 1970s and has been reignited by the current state of US media and politics.

JESSICA HOPSICKER was twenty-one when she interviewed Hunter Thompson and is still somewhat shell-shocked from it. She now works in a cemetery in Cincinnati, and sometimes as a professional pirate. She is writing two books simultaneously while digging herself out of a mountain of student-loan debt.

THE LAST INTERVIEW SERIES

MARTIN LUTHER KING, JR.: THE LAST INTERVIEW

"Inustice anywhere is a threat to justice everywhere."

$15.99 / $21.99 CAN
978-1-61219-616-9
ebook: 978-1-61219-617-6

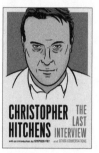

CHRISTOPHER HITCHENS: THE LAST INTERVIEW

"If someone says I'm doing this out of faith, I say, Why don't you do it out of conviction?"

$15.99 / $20.99 CAN
978-1-61219-672-5
ebook: 978-1-61219-673-2

THE LAST INTERVIEW SERIES

NORA EPHRON: THE LAST INTERVIEW

"You better *make* them care about what you think. It had better be quirky or perverse or thoughtful enough so that you hit some chord in them. Otherwise, it doesn't work."

$15.95 / $20.95 CAN
978-1-61219-524-7
ebook: 978-1-61219-525-4

JANE JACOBS: THE LAST INTERVIEW

"I would like it to be understood that all our human economic achievements have been done by ordinary people, not by exceptionally educated people, or by elites, or by supernatural forces."

$15.95 / $20.95 CAN
978-1-61219-534-6
ebook: 978-1-61219-535-3

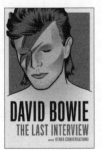

DAVID BOWIE: THE LAST INTERVIEW

"I have no time for glamour. It seems a ridiculous thing to strive for... A clean pair of shoes should serve quite well."

$16.99 / $22.99 CAN
978-1-61219-575-9
ebook: 978-1-61219-576-6

THE LAST INTERVIEW SERIES

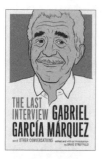

GABRIEL GÁRCIA MÁRQUEZ: THE LAST INTERVIEW

"The only thing the Nobel Prize is good for is not having to wait in line."

$15.95 / $15.95 CAN
978-1-61219-480-6
ebook: 978-1-61219-481-3

LOU REED: THE LAST INTERVIEW

"Hubert Selby. William Burroughs. Allen Ginsberg. Delmore Schwartz... I thought if you could do what those writers did and put it to drums and guitar, you'd have the greatest thing on earth."

$15.95 / $15.95 CAN
978-1-61219-478-3
ebook: 978-1-61219-479-0

ERNEST HEMINGWAY: THE LAST INTERVIEW

"The most essential gift for a good writer is a built-in, shockproof, shit detector."

$15.95 / $20.95 CAN
978-1-61219-522-3
ebook: 978-1-61219-523-0

PHILIP K. DICK: THE LAST INTERVIEW

"The basic thing is, how frightened are you of chaos? And how happy are you with order?"

$15.95 / $20.95 CAN
978-1-61219-526-1
ebook: 978-1-61219-527-8

THE LAST INTERVIEW SERIES

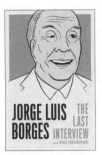

JORGE LUIS BORGES: THE LAST INTERVIEW

"Believe me: the benefits of blindness have been greatly exaggerated. If I could see, I would never leave the house, I'd stay indoors reading the many books that surround me."

translated by KIT MAUDE

$15.95 / $15.95 CAN
978-1-61219-204-8
ebook: 978-1-61219-205-5

HANNAH ARENDT: THE LAST INTERVIEW

"There are no dangerous thoughts for the simple reason that thinking itself is such a dangerous enterprise."

$15.95 / $15.95 CAN
978-1-61219-311-3
ebook: 978-1-61219-312-0

RAY BRADBURY: THE LAST INTERVIEW

"You don't have to destroy books to destroy a culture. Just get people to stop reading them."

$15.95 / $15.95 CAN
978-1-61219-421-9
ebook: 978-1-61219-422-6

JAMES BALDWIN: THE LAST INTERVIEW

"You don't realize that you're intelligent until it gets you into trouble."

$15.95 / $15.95 CAN
978-1-61219-400-4
ebook: 978-1-61219-401-1

THE LAST INTERVIEW SERIES

KURT VONNEGUT: THE LAST INTERVIEW

"I think it can be tremendously refreshing if a creator of literature has something on his mind other than the history of literature so far. Literature should not disappear up its own asshole, so to speak."

$15.95 / $17.95 CAN
978-1-61219-090-7
ebook: 978-1-61219-091-4

LEARNING TO LIVE FINALLY: THE LAST INTERVIEW
JACQUES DERRIDA

"I am at war with myself, it's true, you couldn't possibly know to what extent . . . I say contradictory things that are, we might say, in real tension; they are what construct me, make me live, and will make me die."

translated by PASCAL-ANNE BRAULT and MICHAEL NAAS

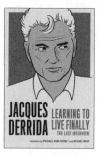

$15.95 / $17.95 CAN
978-1-61219-094-5
ebook: 978-1-61219-032-7

ROBERTO BOLAÑO: THE LAST INTERVIEW

"Posthumous: It sounds like the name of a Roman gladiator, an unconquered gladiator. At least that's what poor Posthumous would like to believe. It gives him courage."

translated by SYBIL PEREZ and others

$15.95 / $17.95 CAN
978-1-61219-095-2
ebook: 978-1-61219-033-4

DAVID FOSTER WALLACE: THE LAST INTERVIEW

"I don't know what you're thinking or what it's like inside you and you don't know what it's like inside me. In fiction . . . we can leap over that wall itself in a certain way."

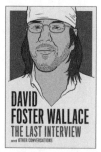

$15.95 / $15.95 CAN
978-1-61219-206-2
ebook: 978-1-61219-207-9